HOW TO BUILD AND FURNISH

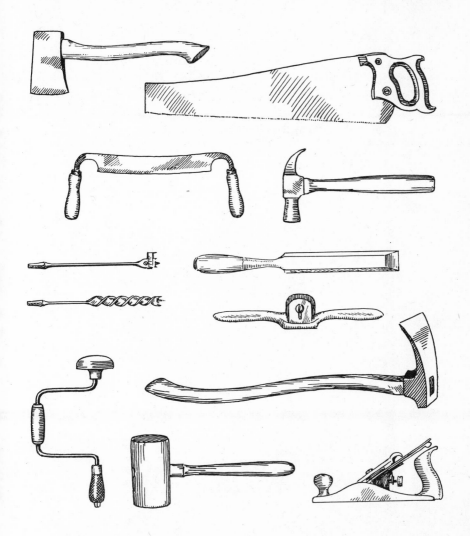

A LOG CABIN

Other Works By W. Ben Hunt

American Indian Beadwork
Ben Hunt's Big Book of Whittling
Ben Hunt's Big Indiancraft Book
Indian Leathercraft
One Hundred One Alphabets (Coauthor, Ed. C. Hunt)

HOW TO BUILD AND FURNISH A LOG CABIN

THE EASY-NATURAL WAY USING ONLY HAND TOOLS AND THE WOODS AROUND YOU

W. BEN HUNT

COLLIER BOOKS
A Division of Macmillan Publishing Co., Inc.
NEW YORK
COLLIER MACMILLAN PUBLISHERS
LONDON

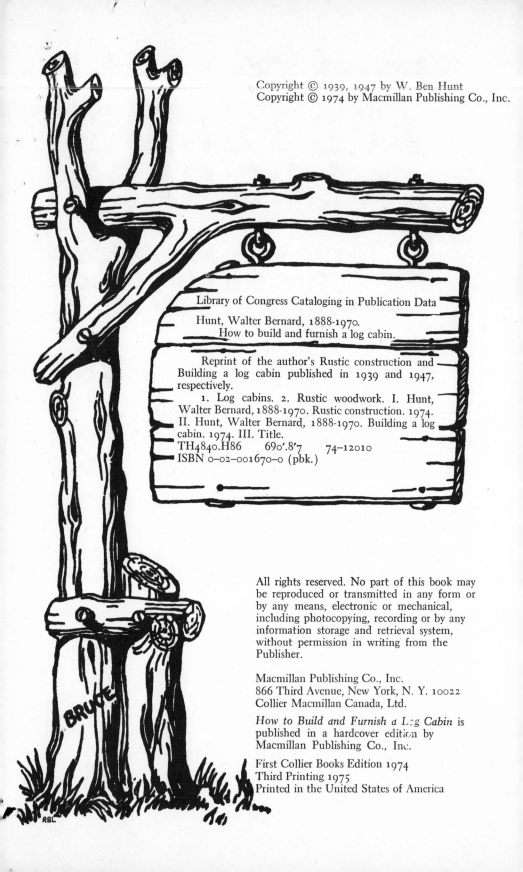

Library of Congress Cataloging in Publication Data

Hunt, Walter Bernard, 1888-1970.
    How to build and furnish a log cabin.

    Reprint of the author's Rustic construction and
Building a log cabin published in 1939 and 1947,
respectively.
    1. Log cabins. 2. Rustic woodwork. I. Hunt,
Walter Bernard, 1888-1970. Rustic construction. 1974.
II. Hunt, Walter Bernard, 1888-1970. Building a log
cabin. 1974. III. Title.
TH4840.H86   690'.8'7   74–12010
ISBN 0–02–001670–0 (pbk.)

Macmillan Publishing Co., Inc.
866 Third Avenue, New York, N. Y. 10022
Collier Macmillan Canada, Ltd.

How to Build and Furnish a Log Cabin is
published in a hardcover edition by
Macmillan Publishing Co., Inc.

First Collier Books Edition 1974
Third Printing 1975
Printed in the United States of America

CONTENTS

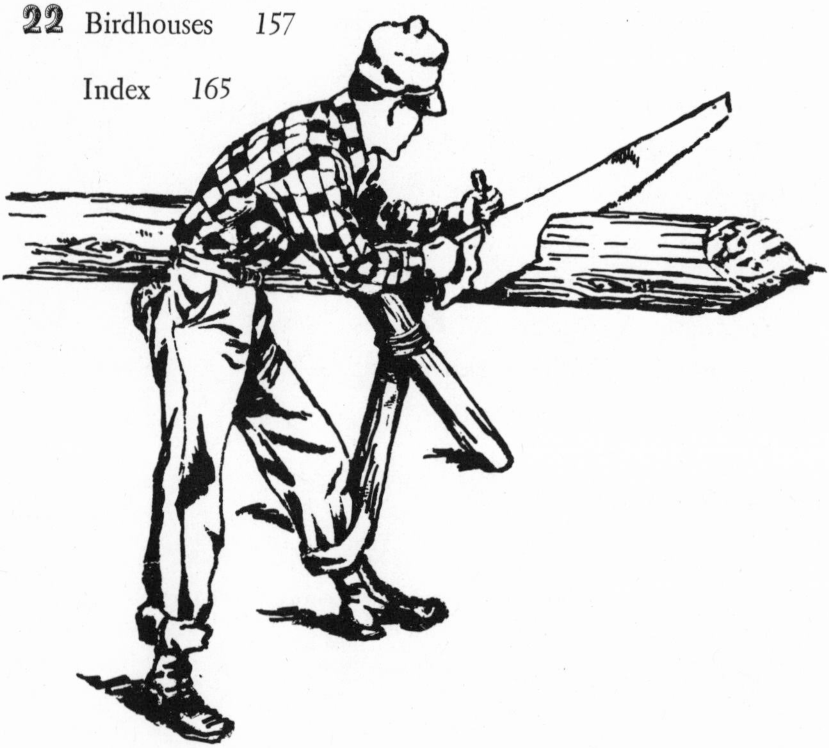

FOREWORD

W. Ben Hunt was born in Wisconsin about ninety years ago. Most of his life was spent in teaching, creating artwork, writing, and lecturing about the out-of-doors. He was a self-taught expert on the crafts of the Plains and Woodland Indians, and he wrote about, and for, scouts of all ages.

How to Build and Furnish a Log Cabin is a compilation of two of Ben Hunt's books: *Building a Log Cabin*, first published in 1947, and *Rustic Construction*, first published in 1939. Both of these books are reproduced exactly as they first appeared, with the drawings and photographs that W. Ben Hunt produced and selected for the original editions.

Even if you live in a city or suburb, you've probably thought of owning a rustic cabin: a place all alone by the quiet of a lake, or snuggled in the side of a mountain. A primitive but cozy den, complete with a warm fireplace and dancing shadows.

Our forefathers built homes using the woods around them and furnishing them with slab furniture. They built durable, dry, windproof, strong, and protective dwellings using only hand tools. You can do it, too.

In this day of power saws, lumberyards, and constantly rising prices, perhaps it is good to think back on a simpler time when the bark was left on the trees, and tables, chairs, and beds were fashioned from split half-logs.

We believe that W. Ben Hunt would be delighted if everyone would try his hand at truly rustic construction. But if you're not ready for an entire cabin, you can content yourself with small items such as lamps, fences, candlesticks, and gates. So, take saw, hand ax, adz, hammer, cant hood, gage, and plane in hand, go out into the forest, and make the woods work for you.

Editor
1974

INTRODUCTION TO LOG CABIN CONSTRUCTION

This book is the outgrowth of the author's own experience in log-cabin construction. It was suggested by the many questions about the subject put to him the past few years by prospective builders and other interested persons. To encourage and assist such individuals this work is expressly written.

When we speak of the pioneer log cabin we commonly think of a small dwelling with a large fireplace for cooking, a puncheon or padded clay floor, etc. Built often in great haste, it had few comforts. But because the log cabin truly reflected the materials and tools and the way of life of the builders, it had genuine architectural beauty. The cabin that you are going to build will be exactly like it in many of its details.

In this book we shall be concerned primarily with the smaller type of cabin such as might be used for a summer home, a clubhouse, or perhaps a rustic home of very modest size. The more pretentious type of structure, such as the large lodge and elaborate home, is essentially similar in construction but would require detailed explanation by an experienced architect. Here fundamentals are stressed. With the methods described in the pages that follow even the inexperienced person can build himself an ordinary cabin without great trouble, if he is willing to learn how to use a saw, ax, and adz with some degree of proficiency.

The emphasis throughout is on the simplest, most practical methods that will produce the best results. The drawings show all important points and by themselves almost tell the whole story.

It is the sincere hope of the author that this work will be a real help to his fellow admirers of the heritage of which the log cabin is a part. If they derive as much pleasure and satisfaction out of building and using their own log cabin as he has, his efforts will be more than amply rewarded.

W. B. H.

LOG CABIN CONSTRUCTION

THE CABIN
AND THE SITE

THE CABIN

The log cabin is a product of the woods and forest. A log cabin should appear to have grown out of the soil on which it stands. It belongs in the country and preferably near a woods. This type of structure would be absolutely out of place in the city surrounded by modern, up-to-date houses or on a skimpy, poorly selected piece of land. Properly constructed and located, the beauty of the log cabin is unique.

The simplest cabin is a one-room structure (Fig. 1). To this a porch can be added. For use as a sleeping porch or dining room during the summer months this addition can be screened and fitted with canvas drops. The porch will also serve as a convenient storage place for firewood if you plan to use your log cabin during the winter months.

Should you be in need of extra room, a lean-to kitchen such as that shown in Figure 2 built against one end will be of help. This ought to be made of logs but if necessary slabs or boards will be found satisfactory. If constructed large enough, it can be used as a bedroom.

The three-room cabin shown in Figure 3 will accommodate two to three people as a permanent dwelling. Clothes closets, cabinets, shelves, and so on will, of course, have to be added as and where needed.

Naturally the log cabins which are being erected today generally are not as primitive as those of the early settlers. Cabins are being built with some or all modern conveniences—heating, plumbing, and lighting. These features, which really require the services of architects and contractors, will be considered briefly later on.

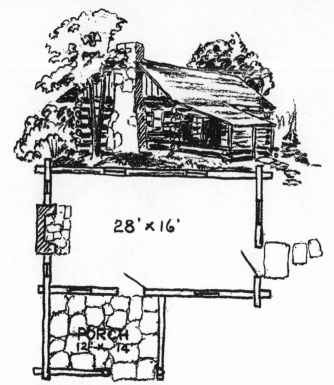

Fig. 1. One-room cabin.

Fig. 2. One-room cabin with lean-to kitchen.

THE SITE

The finest log cabin will be a failure if it is not favorably located. Hence, in selecting the site for your cabin, thoughtful consideration must be given to the following factors: drainage, water supply, orientation, accessibility, and safety. When building in the city, municipal laws, enacted to protect the citizens from danger and disease, allow no alternatives in these matters. However, the builder usually does not encounter such rules and restrictions in rural areas. The initiative is left to you, then, to provide for the health and safety of your family and your friends.

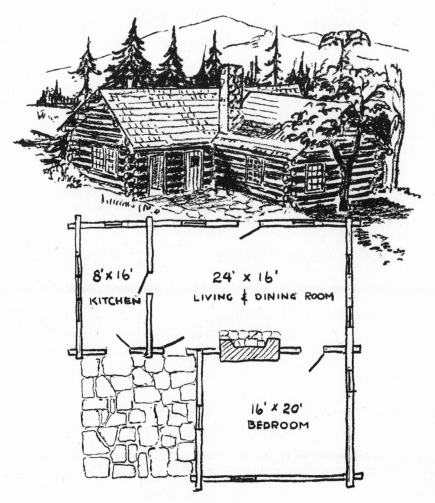

Fig. 3. Three-room cabin.

Drainage

The log cabin must be built on high solid ground. Whether you build in the woods, the mountains, along some river or lake good drainage away from the building is essential. Low land should be avoided whenever possible.

Good drainage or slope is essential to the proper functioning of the sewerage system. Septic tanks are very effective for the sanitary disposal of sewerage. Naturally, a septic tank must be lower than the house drains and at the same time cannot be set in low, wet ground because the effluent must drain off into the soil. In a properly built septic tank this effluent is crystal clear. Too often, however, the overflow is drained into a creek or river. There should be no visible overflow if the tank is correctly constructed and placed in sandy or gravel soil. An installation of this type usually operates without trouble for from ten to fifteen years. After this time the tank may have to be cleaned out and new laterals may have to be dug for the overflow.

Water Supply

A clean, pure water supply must be available. In the city, water is supplied and carefully watched but in small towns and in the country it must be obtained from springs and wells.

Perhaps there is a spring on your lot. This may be your answer if there is enough of a flow. A springhouse can be erected over it and the water can be piped or pumped into the house, depending on the lay of the land. The springhouse can be used as a cooler during the summer months.

You may prefer a dug well. Dug wells are lined with stone and the water generally seeps in from the bottom because they are dug down to a level at which water is found. These wells should be covered with a tight cement or board top that has a trap door for hauling up water. A hand pump, too, can be installed.

A driven well is very satisfactory. It is made with a well point, Figure 4, which is a perforated section of pipe with a steel point at the lower

STANDARD TYPE

FOR STONY SOIL

Fig. 4. Well points.

Top: Trapper's cabin in the Rockies.
Center left: Square-hewn log cabin in the Ozarks.
Center right: Old pioneer cabin of walnut logs
in Wisconsin. **Bottom:** Mud dauber and
builder in Ouachita Mountains.

Cabin of square-hewn oak logs. The author spent
his boyhood days here.

end. To the upper end, sections of pipe are coupled and the point is
driven into the soil. Additional sections are joined to this pipe as it is
driven down until water is reached. A hand pump is used to draw the
water to the surface. There are two types of points, one for ordinary
and sandy soil and one for rocky soil.

Drilled wells are the best source of water supply and, of course, are
more expensive than the others. They are usually termed deep wells.
Gas or electric pumps can be used in connection with them. With a
pumping system and a good sewerage disposal system the log cabin has
some of the basic conveniences of a modern city home.

Orientation

Careful thought should be given to the direction in which the cabin
is to face. The chief points to be taken into consideration are commonly designated as sunlight, prevailing winds during the various seasons, and the view.

In general, when you speak of view in the city the word has reference to the houses in the immediate vicinity. In the country, however, you take into consideration a different type of surrounding. You look for scenery most of all. If you are just starting out in life you can, within a few years, grow a lot of your own scenery. It takes about ten years for trees and shrubs to grow large enough to shut out a part of the landscape that may be an eyesore. With planned planting, in about twenty years you can have anything you have ever wished for. The open side of your home should be bright and cheerful and if your lot is large enough you will be able to plant so that there will be a pleasant view from every window.

It should be noted that excessive shade is not good for log cabins. The logs usually are unpainted and therefore should have a chance to dry out after rains. A cabin in a pretty shaded nook may sound and look fine, but it will become damp and uncomfortable without adequate sunlight and air. Moss in its proper place is beautiful; as far as the log cabin is concerned it does not make for human comfort.

Accessibility

It is always advantageous to build in the vicinity of a highway, especially if your cabin is to be used during the winter. However, do not get too close to a main road because of the constant rush of traffic. Side roads are fine if they are kept open. If one has to get to work on time, however, it isn't very enjoyable to have to sit and wait for the snowplow after each storm. If you are going to use your cabin during the summer months only, you need not worry about snow and sleet. For a year-round home this is an important consideration. It might not be a bad idea, then, to see your prospective site at its worst, that is, during the winter. Remember, too, that your own driveway will cause more trouble than the highway unless you plow it yourself or are able to arrange to have it plowed.

The immediate entrance to your cabin, that is, the driveway, deserves practical consideration. Money and time are required to build a driveway over low, swampy land. A hillside drive also involves a lot of bother and expense until it is packed down. If not laid correctly, the danger of washouts is always present. Moreover, such an approach can be hazardous in winter.

The proximity of churches, schools, stores, doctors, post office, bus lines, and so on, should be carefully studied in terms of your own situation.

Safety

Finally, do not overlook the safety factor in the selection of your site. Nearness of cliffs, means of escape in case of forest fire, protection from floods and storms—all of these are taken into account by the circumspect builder.

LOGS AND OTHER MATERIALS

LOGS

Sources of Logs

Sometimes logs can be obtained on or near the site. As a general rule, however, they will have to be procured elsewhere. Usually logs are bought from someone who has a good stand of timber. Often he will cut them and haul them for you. Sometimes they can be purchased from a saw mill or lumber company.

Kinds of Logs

You will be most fortunate if you obtain precisely what you are looking for in the way of logs. In some parts of the country obtaining them is not much of a problem; in others it is. There are cabins in Wisconsin built of logs shipped from the west coast. Sometimes a local telephone or electric power company will supply them. From a practical standpoint, electric-line poles are about the best that can be obtained as they usually are of straight, peeled cedar and have little taper.

Balsam, spruce, and white pine make excellent log cabins and are easy to work. Tamarack, if used the summer after it is cut, is also easy to work. This wood, however, is very hard when dry. Still it is often used because of its durability. The first section of my cabin was built of local tamarack. Put up some twenty-odd years ago, it still is as sound as a dollar. Poplar will last a long time if it is kept off the ground.

Although some logs naturally are easier to work than others, still, in the days when log cabins were built not so much for atmosphere as for protection from the atmosphere, the builders used whatever logs were handy. The principal requirements are that logs be straight and not have too many branches. It is difficult work to peel logs that had many branches, especially if the knots are on the inside. It is not easy to drawknife these knots and as a rule they must be chopped off smooth with an ax. It is better to use mixed logs, that is, logs of different kinds, than to use one kind if some are crooked or have too much taper.

You will also need some small logs for rafters. These are usually about half the size of the wall logs, but should be the straightest ones available.

Ordering Logs

Knowing the size of your cabin and the average size of the logs available you can determine almost to the foot how many logs you will need. By the average size of log is meant the diameter of the log at the center. Thus a log measuring 14 in. at the butt and 8 in. at the top will average 11 in. To determine the number of logs of the size required you can draw each side elevated to scale figuring the logs 11 in. in diameter the full length of the cabin. A few extra logs should be ordered, however.

Seasoning Logs

Ideally, logs should be fully dried, or seasoned, to prevent checking or cracking. There is no treatment, however, that will completely eliminate this difficulty. The logs should be peeled and then racked up so that they will not touch each other after which they are covered with hay or straw to protect them from the sun (Fig. 5). They should be allowed to stand this way for at least six months, and if possible, a year. When building is started, the inside surface of the logs should be

Fig. 5. Logs laid out for seasoning.

"As though it grew out of the soil on which it stands."

drawknifed if they are to be oiled or stained later. This operation is performed usually as each log goes into place. It is hard work to clean the logs after they have been laid up and chinked.

OTHER BUILDING MATERIALS

While logs are the first requirement on the list of materials, other important items deserve brief consideration. You will also need sand, gravel, stone, and cement. These, of course, can be purchased from your local dealer. For your fireplace you will also have to obtain firebrick. Then there are windows, doors, roofing and flooring boards, and shingles. Your materials will also include an ample supply of oakum and plaster for chinking. Planking 2 by 6 or 2 by 8 in. will be needed for door and window frames and floor joists.

It is important that good washed sand and gravel be used for all concrete work. Be on guard against material containing dirt or clay because it will not withstand the weather. Do not line your fireplace with stone, which may explode from the heat. Use good firebrick set in fire clay. More will be said about fireplaces later. Then, also, buy your windows before you put up the walls so that you can determine the exact width and length of the frames. Doors can be made to fit any opening if you build them yourself. If not, also buy your doors first, or you can have special doors made by a millwork company.

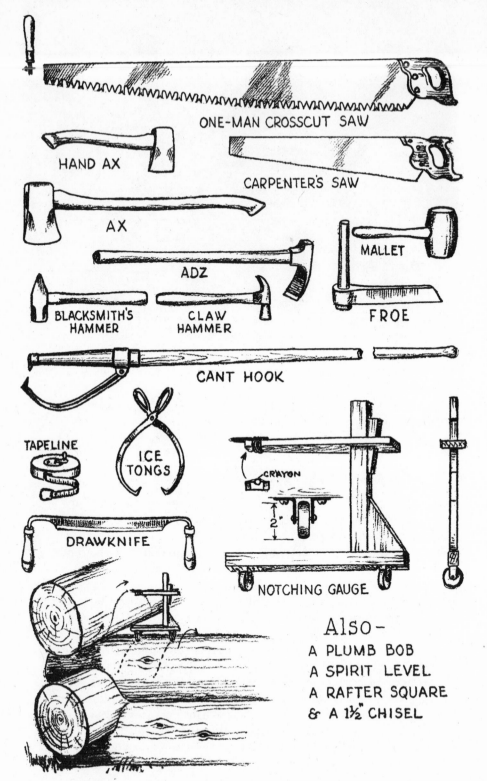

ONE-MAN CROSSCUT SAW

HAND AX

CARPENTER'S SAW

AX

ADZ

MALLET

BLACKSMITH'S HAMMER

CLAW HAMMER

FROE

CANT HOOK

TAPELINE

ICE TONGS

CRAYON

2"

NOTCHING GAUGE

DRAWKNIFE

Also—
A PLUMB BOB
A SPIRIT LEVEL
A RAFTER SQUARE
& A 1½" CHISEL

Fig. 6. Tools used for log cabin construction.

TOOLS

In the pioneer days probably many log cabins were built with only an ax and a saw. Much labor and great skill certainly were required to build a good structure with such limitations. Today the worker has at his disposal a variety of high-grade tools that will make his labor simpler, more pleasant, and more effective (Fig. 6).

A 4½- or 5-ft., one- or two-man crosscut saw is indispensable, and the regular handsaw, of course, can always be used. Then you will need a hand ax. This is a very important tool and should be of good steel to keep an edge. A large ax may be useful at times but can be dispensed with, unless you wish to chop the ends of the logs. An adz is an excellent tool for hewing, but it is very dangerous in the hands of an inexperienced workman. In fact, it is dangerous at all times and must be used with caution. A broad ax will do the same work on straight cuts. However, if you have neither an adz nor a broad ax the little squaring or leveling that has to be done can be taken care of with a hand ax. You will also need a drawknife. If possible the blade should be longer than that of the ordinary drawknife. One that is used for shingles is the best for this type of work, especially if the logs are large. It will save many a bruised knuckle. Hammers you have, and if you have ever tried to drive a 60-penny spike with a claw hammer you will know that a heavier one will be a lot easier to work with. Hence, a small blacksmith's hammer is recommended. Another tool that should be mentioned, but with which few people are acquainted, is the froe (Figs. 6 and 43). This tool was formerly and most likely still is used for splitting shingles. A heavy wooden mallet is used to drive it into the wood. A

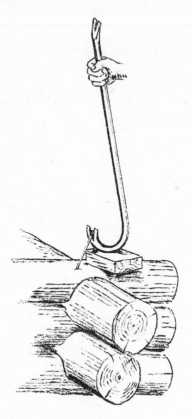

Fig. 7. Wrecking bar.

large, heavy chisel and a gouge will often come in handy. The gouge should be ground on the inside, or concave, surface.

A cant hook is generally used by woodsmen for handling logs, but the author discovered that a couple of ice tongs are excellent substitutes for log-cabin construction. They are very handy for lifting and carrying logs.

You will notice the notching gauge in Figure 6. It is very effective for accurate matching. However, you will have to make it yourself. A dividers can be used as a notching gauge but it is not as accurate. Logs that are marked and cut out carefully will fit perfectly. The cut along the line is made with a large gouge and the rest of the wood is cut away with an ax or adz.

A level, plumb bob, large square, and perhaps a wrecking bar will also be used. The last mentioned will be found useful for pulling out spikes and prying apart logs that have to be changed (Fig. 7). A good tapeline and other rules will be required at all times. Be sure that some good black or blue marking crayon is included in your list of materials.

All tools must be sharp if you want a nice-looking cabin. Ax and drawknife cuts that show ridges and roughness present a very displeasing appearance. There is no such thing, then, as a tool that is too sharp. For this reason you should have sharpening stones handy at all times. A good grindstone will be found best for axes, adzes, chisels, and drawknives. There is no danger of burning tools and destroying their temper if they are sharpened on a grindstone. No motor is required. An emery or carborundum wheel can be used by those who are not acquainted with or who do not know how to use a grindstone, but unless such wheels are at least 6 in. in diameter there is the danger of grinding large cutting tools too hollow. A small oilstone or a whetstone will be found best for the finished edge. A couple of files—a flat-mill file and triangular file for saws—should be on hand also.

There are two ways of caring for tools. One is to go over them and hone or sharpen them before going to work each day, or to do this in the evening after work. If time is taken out to sharpen tools during working hours the progress of your helpers will be retarded. It might be a good gesture, then, to have your tools ready for use before work is begun.

FOUNDATIONS AND FIREPLACES

PREPARING THE SITE

Whether you build on level ground or on a hillside, you will have to prepare the site. If trees must be cut down, be sure to grub out the roots—especially if they will interfere with the foundation. While a cabin that is to be erected on flat land presents no particular problem at this point, a hillside house must be protected from the wash of rains. So if your tract has considerable slope, study the situation carefully and build a retaining wall or watershed as required. You will be certain then of a dry basement or, on the other hand, a dry floor.

FOUNDATIONS

Three types of foundations may be distinguished: piers, foundation walls, and basements. You will probably use the first mentioned because they are easy to make and are generally quite satisfactory. For all types, a mixture of stone and concrete is recommended.

Piers

Concrete piers can be set about 6 ft. apart. They should reach down to firm ground beneath the frost line. Figure 8 shows their construction. The ground makes the form for the lower portion and a board frame for the part above the ground. A chalk line stretched level is used to determine the height. Cabins should be set low as a rule at the highest spot of the site. The tops of the piers should be only a few inches above the ground. Sometimes the piers are tapered toward the top. This is commonly done if they are set in loose soil.

A recommended mixture for concrete is 1 part of Portland cement, 2 of washed sand, and 2 to 4 of gravel. If you have never mixed concrete, it should be pointed out that dry material is easier to work than moist material. The cement must be dry. Now, by a part is meant, as a general rule, a shovelful. Hence, the proportions would be 1 shovelful of cement, 2 shovelsful of sand, and so on.

Concrete can be mixed in a large or small mortar box with 6- or 8-in. sides. For small quantities a metal wheelbarrow may be practical. The ingredients are added in the following order: gravel, sand, cement. The material is then worked or mixed by shoveling back and forth until it shows an even color. Water is now added gradually until the mixture attains working consistency. It should be neither too thin nor too thick. Concrete for laying up stone should be somewhat richer. A mixture of about 1 part cement to 3 parts of sand is advisable. Rocks and stone can be used as a filler for any type of wall.

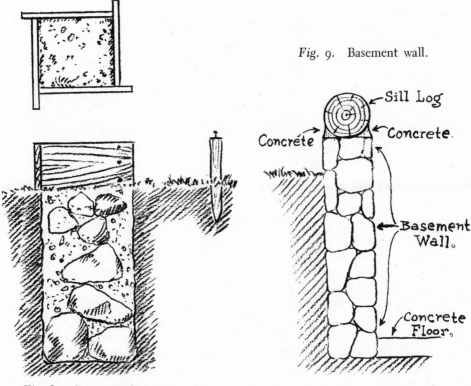

Fig. 9. Basement wall.

Sill Log

Concrete

Concrete

Basement Wall.

Concrete Floor.

Fig. 8. Concrete pier.

Foundation Walls and Basement

Either foundation walls or a basement, if storage space is necessary, will very likely be built if your log cabin is to be used as a permanent home. These, however, are difficult to construct so that you will do well to hire a contractor to build them for you. In the end you will be time and money ahead.

If you decide to erect a foundation wall, be sure to provide openings, 6 to 12 in. square, for ventilation. These vents are to be covered with ¼- or ½-in. screen to keep out small animals. I have been awakened more than once by a rumpus under my cabin. Usually a weasel or a mink chases a rabbit and corners him down there. They can kick up quite a fuss. The vents should be made so that they can be entirely closed during the winter.

Since bare concrete in connection with a log cabin does not present too pleasant an appearance, you might do well to face the exposed surface of the foundation walls with stone, which will blend well with the logs.

Under ordinary conditions it is not necessary to provide for anchoring the sill logs to the piers or foundation walls. However, if you are building in an area where tornadoes and violent storms are known to occur it might be advisable to set bolts into the top of your foundation. The decision is up to the individual builder.

For a basement, the walls are built like any other walls with enough surface at the top to allow for a cement or plaster edge along the sill log (Fig. 9). This is designed to shed water. It is a good idea to creosote the sill logs if they rest on piers below the floor level. Creosote has a rather strong odor which is quite offensive to some people. Therefore, although it is an excellent preservative, it should be used below or directly over the ground.

THE FIREPLACE

A log cabin would not be a log cabin without a fireplace. There are any number of effective designs for fireplaces. If you study a few you can plan one of your own. Although I recommend that you have a mason do the actual work, it is important that you understand the basic principles of fireplace construction.

The base of the fireplace must be sturdy because it will have to support a great weight of stone. It must reach below the frost line, just as the piers. If there is a basement, the base of the fireplace will be part of the foundation and the hearth can be built up between the floor joists as in any other home. In case there is no basement, of course, a hole will have to be dug. The base is built up to within about 4 in. of

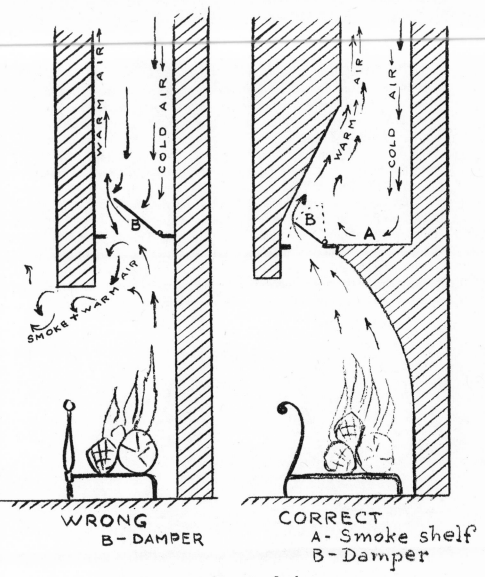

WARM AIR — COLD AIR

B

SMOKE + WARM AIR

WRONG
B — DAMPER

WARM AIR — COLD AIR

B — A

CORRECT
A - Smoke shelf
B - Damper

Fig. 10. Correct and incorrect fireplace construction.

the floor level. Large stones are used for filler and rods for reinforcement. A wood form, of course, will have to be used for the section above the ground.

Figure 10 shows the correct design of a fireplace to obtain proper draft. This basic construction is requisite for a fireplace to draw well and throw out heat. The smoke is carried by the warm air through the throat and up the flue. Note that the cold air seeks its way down the flue but that the smoke shelf prevents it from forcing smoke into the room by deflecting it upward. The damper helps to throw the cold downdraft of the flue upward. When the fireplace is not in use the damper is closed to prevent unwelcome visitors from entering the cabin.

A sheet-iron fireplace unit is shown in Figure 11. Various makes are on the market and may be obtained from larger hardware dealers and firms specializing in fireplace equipment. Stone and brick can be masoned around it. Hot-air registers at the top and the bottom throw added heat into the room.

There are different methods of building up the chimney. One is to allow a gap in the logs as the walls are erected and then to build the fireplace and chimney into that space (Fig. 12). The fireplace is then built into the opening as in Figure 13. In this case the chimney will be on the outside. Another method is simpler to my way of thinking. It consists of building up the entire fireplace and chimney before the walls or any logs are laid. Obviously the workmen have much more

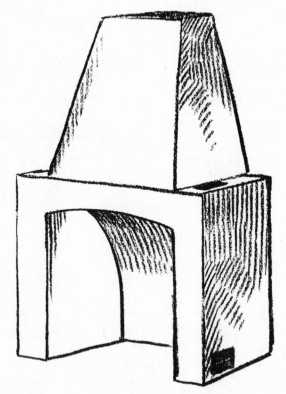

Fig. 11. Sheet-iron fireplace unit.

Fig. 12. Opening for fireplace.

Fig. 13. Fireplace built into opening such
as shown in Fig. 12. The chimney will be
outside.

23

Fig. 14. Fireplace with sides grooved for logs.

freedom. A groove is left down the sides of the chimney into which the ends of the logs are fitted (Fig. 14). It is much easier to get the ends of the logs into this recess than to fit the chimney to the logs. If the chimney is built last, the projecting logs must be cut to shape at the opening and must be held in place by a couple of heavy planks (Fig. 12). Some builders construct the walls and fireplace simultaneously.

The fireplace can be faced on all sides with cut stone, flagstone, round boulders, or brick. Your selection will depend on the material available and your individual preferences. Common brick, new or old, makes a fine fireplace for a log cabin. Split field stone seems to be everyone's choice, but it must be laid up correctly to look right. The use of stones of several contrasting colors does not produce a very beautiful effect. It is much better to use different shades of one color, whether they run to grays or browns or whatever is to be had in your locality.

Chimney erected and sill logs in place.

One method of building the roof around the chimney.

A gaudy fireplace is just as out of place in a log cabin as chromium or crystal lighting fixtures.

The fireplace proper, that is, the place where the fire will be, is to be lined with firebrick set in fire clay. Stones should not be used because with the extreme changes in temperature they flake off and often explode. In some localities native stone is especially lacking in heat-resisting qualities.

The hearth, the floor of the fireplace, is laid after the floor of the cabin. It is usually set in concrete. A layer of rather "dry" mixed cement is laid over the entire area and flagstones or other flat stones are set level with the floor. A 3 to 1 mortar is poured and troweled between them. Brick also can be used and will provide a fine level surface.

In Figure 13 the chimney is on the outside of the cabin. The chimney of the fireplace on this page is visible both on the inside and the outside. Some chimneys of this type are built wide enough to occupy the better portion of the wall area.

WALLS

By this time your tract will have been cleared and the foundation (piers, foundation wall, or basement) built. The fireplace, if you have followed the author's recommendation, now stands high above the site and you are ready to begin the most intriguing part of the job, laying up the logs.

SILL AND END LOGS

First of all the logs should be spread out on the ground so that you can see them all. Much time and effort is saved if you are able to select them as you need them without turning over the entire pile. Pick out the two largest and straightest for the sill logs, that is, the first logs for the long sides, and lay them on the piers or foundation wall. The butts should be at opposite ends. In other words, if the butt end of one faces north, the other should face south. Note well that as the walls are built, the butt ends are to be alternated in this manner so that the walls will be level. The logs, of course, are cut out flat where they rest on the piers to provide a firm frame on which to build. For foundation walls the sill logs are hewed flat the full length of the surface on which they are to rest. With the two sill logs placed solidly on the foundation, the end logs are now notched to them and laid in place. There is a space equal to the thickness of a half log between these logs and the tops of the piers (Fig. 15). To prevent sagging, the tops of the piers under these logs are built up to the logs with concrete.

The floor joists can be laid either before or after the walls (see Chap. 8, Floors, Stairs, and Ceilings). It is advisable to build the floor last because while working on the inside, joists are very much in the way. Walking over them is troublesome and laying loose boards over them is dangerous. You will be better off, therefore, leaving the ground to walk on until the walls are built. The debris, incidentally, will be more easily removed. Of course, if there is a basement below the house, joists and a subfloor must be laid before the walls are put up, as in any other building.

JOINTS

Many different methods of joining logs are used in log-cabin construction. Some are employed for their appearance. Others are preferred for strength and economy. Only a few basic ones will be described here.

A-and-V Joint

The A-and-V joint shown in Figure 16 is recommended for small logs. A minimum of wood is removed with the result that the projecting ends are not unduly weakened. The entire joint is made with a hand ax. The lower log is spiked after it has been cut out.

Common Joint

The common method of notching logs for an accurate fit is shown in Figure 17. It is rather simple. Examine the log so that the best side or face will be on the inside of the cabin. Then mark both sides and both ends with a marking gauge. As shown in Figure 6, the gauge is set to about the middle of the log to be cut if you want the logs to touch, and the arc is marked. If the log is inclined to roll, have someone hold it in place. Now turn the log upside down and cut along this line with a large gouge and mallet to a depth of about an inch and pry away the wood. Then with an ax or adz cut out the remaining wood. A saw cut down the center as shown in Figure 18 will make this operation much simpler. Too much time would be required to complete the notch with a gouge. If you have marked correctly and cut to the line, the log will plop in place like the cover on a trunk. Each corner is secured with a couple of 60-penny nails.

Perhaps you prefer ax-cut ends to saw-cut ends (Fig. 19). The former add a beautiful rustic touch. If you are a good ax man and like such ends it is your privilege to make them. Personally I'll take the saw-cut type because there is less danger of rotting due to absorption of water.

You will observe in some of the drawings that there is space between the logs. Some builders, however, prefer to have the logs touch each other. Whether one method is more advisable than another is a matter

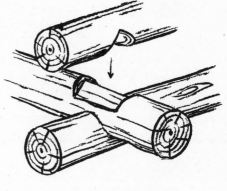

Fig. 15. Sill and end log in place.

Fig. 16. A-and-V joint.

Bottom of log

Fig. 17. Common joint.

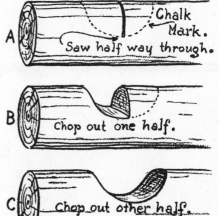

A — Chalk Mark.
Saw half way through.

B — Chop out one half.

C — Chop out other half.

Fig. 18. Method of notching
for common joint.

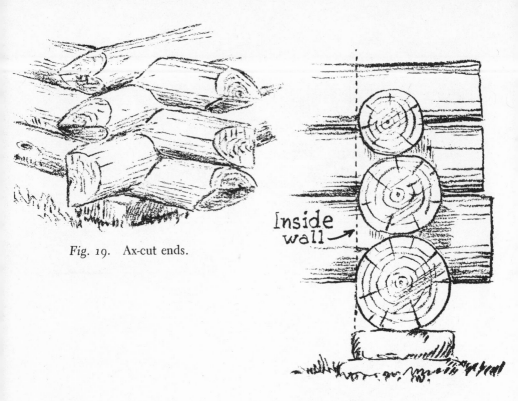

Fig. 19.   Ax-cut ends.

Inside wall →

Fig. 20.   Logs aligned on inside of cabin.

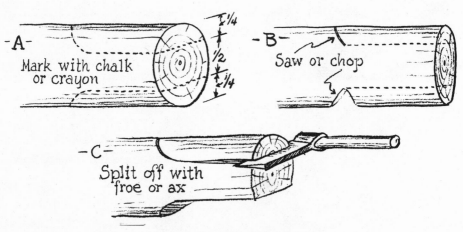

-A-
Mark with chalk
or crayon

¼
½
¼

-B-
Saw or chop

-C-
Split off with
froe or ax

Fig. 21.   Method of cutting dovetail joint.

Left: Laying up walls using the A-and-V joint.
Right: Preparing a common joint with an adz.

of opinion. If space is left between the logs the corners true up better, the walls can be erected faster, and one or two logs can be saved on each wall. These spaces can be filled easily by chinking.

Be sure that the logs on the inside of the wall are in the best possible alignment. Figure 20, while somewhat exaggerated, shows how they should be lined up.

Dovetail Joint

The dovetail joint (Fig. 22) is sometimes used, especially if projecting ends must be eliminated. Sometimes it is used for all corners to save logs. About 2 ft. can be gained on each log with dovetail ends. The procedure for making this joint is shown in Figure 21. First the cutting line is marked off with chalk or crayon. Then a notch is sawed or chopped and the remaining wood is split off with a froe or ax. If the tongue is equal to the thickness of half the log as shown in Figure 21, the logs should touch along their full length provided they are straight. If the tongue is more than half the thickness of the log, there will be a space between the logs. All irregular spots and all knots must be smoothed off with an ax or an adz if the logs are to fit tightly.

Other Methods

Where logs are rather scarce, the method shown in Figure 24 can be employed. This joint eliminates much chopping but it is not as artistic

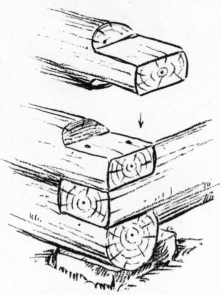

Fig. 22. Dovetail joint.

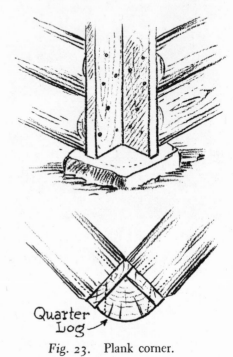

Quarter
Log

Fig. 23. Plank corner.

Fig. 24. Butt joint with logs secured by rods or dowels.

Fig. 25. Sawing out window and door openings.

Fig. 26. Frame nailed to ends of logs.

as those explained above. The logs are held together with long iron rods or hardwood dowels. Inasmuch as no notching is done, the logs must be pinned together with care.

Figure 23 shows another method which makes a very neat corner. For small cabins each of the four walls can be assembled on the ground and then set up, after which the corners are spiked. Care must be taken so that every wall will be absolutely square. This method saves log footage and is faster than any other, for which reason it is practical for auto-camp cottages and the like.

DOOR, WINDOW, AND FIREPLACE OPENINGS

If logs are plentiful, the logs can be built up to the top sill and then the openings for the doors and windows can be cut out. First guide strips are nailed in place as shown in Figure 25. These will also serve as braces to hold the logs in position after they are sawed. Then the frames of 2 by 6- or 2 by 8-in. planks are fitted and nailed into and against the ends of the logs and set in at the bottom as shown in Figure 26. The size of the openings and the frames for the windows will, of course, depend on the dimensions of the sashes, which should be purchased before you start to build.

33

Fireplaces

The logs can be cut to allow necessary openings as the walls are being erected. The opening for a fireplace of the type shown in Figure 13 is illustrated in Figure 12. If the full length of the chimney is to show on the inside of the cabin, the logs are cut from the bottom to the top of the wall. If the fireplace and the chimney are put up first, the logs are cut to fit around it.

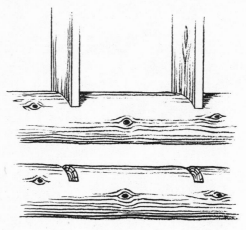

Fig. 27. Frame set into sill log.

Fig. 28. Door frame braced
and ready to be set.

Fig. 29. Door frame set
and properly braced.

Doors

Provision for the openings for the doors is shown in Figures 27, 28, and 29. Slots are cut in the sill log and the lower ends of the door frame are set into them and toenailed. The frames are braced crosswise to keep them square. This type of bracing is shown in Figure 28. Do not remove these braces until all the logs are laid. Two stout supports also should be nailed to the side of the frame as shown in Figure 29 to hold it upright. Be sure that the frame is absolutely plumb. Thus it will act as a true perpendicular guide when laying up the logs because they are aligned with the inner edge of the planks.

Here I would like to insert an important note of caution. Be sure that the log ends which fit against window and door frames are cut square. If only *one* log is cut too short the long 40- or 60-penny spikes will pull the frame out of line. On the other hand, a log that is *too long* will cause a bulge in the frame. A miter-box arrangement as shown in Figure 30 is effective for cutting log ends square. If a log is too short, do not attempt to pull it in place. The frame will be moved out of plumb and a bulge will be produced. The next log may spring out just a bit more and then you will have trouble on your hands. Remember, once frames are in, they are in for good. Frames have the strength to hold a wall rigidly true. For best appearance, the planks should be the same width as the logs or slightly narrower, as shown in Figure 26.

Windows

The walls are now laid up to the level of the window sills. Do not forget to alternate the butt ends.

Now make the window frames as shown in Figure 31. For this purpose 2 by 6- or 2 by 8-in. planks can be used. They are squared up and braced as the door frames were.

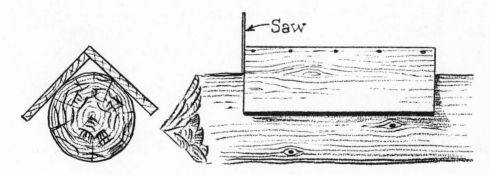

Fig. 30. Guide for cutting log ends square.

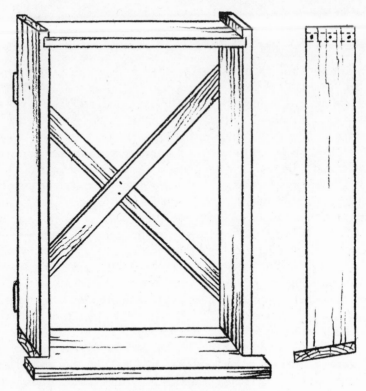

Fig. 31. Braced window frame.

Spikes

Fig. 32. Tops of window and door frames aligned.

To determine the height at which to set the window frames, refer to Figure 32, which shows a door frame and a window frame. As a rule the tops of the windows and doors are at the same level. Thus there will be no break in the log immediately above the door and window openings, which makes for rigid construction. So be governed by the height of the doors. The sill of the window frame sets on or is recessed into the logs depending on dimensions. In the same drawing the log has been cut out to accommodate the window frame.

The frame in Figure 33A fits very accurately. The top meets the log above it as it should. The top plank can be spiked to the upper log. However, an imperfect fit is more likely to occur. In Figure 33B the frame does not reach the upper log. The space A–A in such a case can be filled with a section of log or plaster. In Figure 33C the top log has been cut out for the frame. There should be at least one continuous log above the frames depending on the height of the wall.

If you have the time and energy you can do a little extra trimming around the window and door frames with half logs mitered at the corners. Cedar fence posts often are used for this purpose (see Fig. 34.)

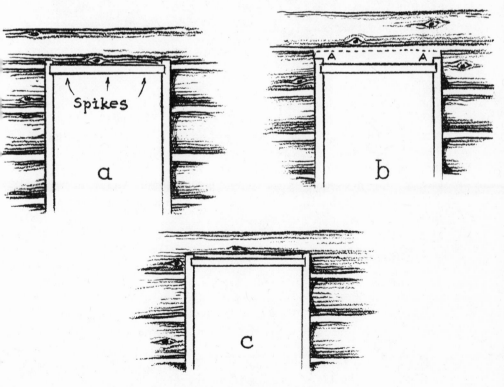

Fig. 33. How window frames may fit.

Laying up walls.

The wall logs may have to be trimmed to fit the half logs. The places where the ends of the wall logs touch should be filled with plaster or cement. Your only problem involved in using half logs is ripping them. They are too small to be ripped in a sawmill and usually are too large for a table saw. Outside of cutting them by hand with a coarse rip saw, the only machine that can be used is a band saw. And if the band saw has a narrow blade, the half logs will require planing to true up the cut.

CEILINGS AND SECOND FLOORS

The walls of small cabins, as a rule, are not built much higher than one log above the tops of the window and door frames. However, one or more logs can be added if higher walls are desired. If there is to be no ceiling proper, that is, if the roof is to constitute the ceiling, you can now proceed to lay the roof rafters.

If a ceiling is to be built as shown in Figure 36, the joists are now notched as in Figure 35 and spiked to the plate logs. Ceiling joists

Fig. 34. Window trim.

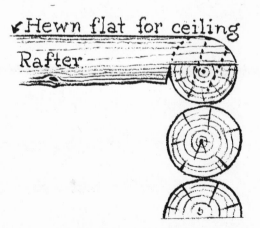

Hewn flat for ceiling
Rafter

Fig. 35. Ceiling rafter notched into plate log.

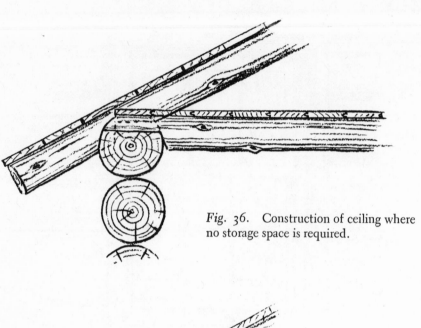

Fig. 36.   Construction of ceiling where no storage space is required.

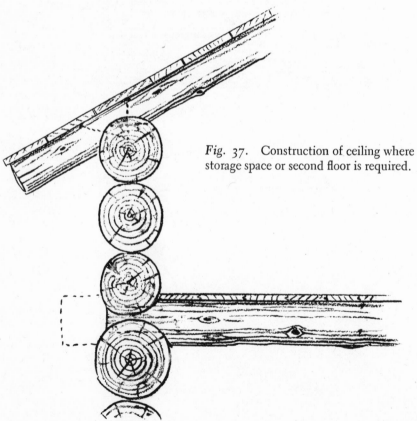

Fig. 37.   Construction of ceiling where storage space or second floor is required.

should be spaced about 18 in. apart to centers if a second story is to be added, or from 3 to 4 ft. apart if they will not have to bear much weight. They are leveled and the ceiling of matched lumber is laid on top of them. The roof is then put on. However, if the wall is one or two logs higher than the level of the ceiling, you will have ample room to lay the floor after the roof is up. The important reason for building the roof before laying the floor, whenever possible, is that even a light shower may permanently warp the floor.

If your cabin is to be a story and a half (Fig. 37) or two stories high, the joists are set, the walls are built up to the desired height, and the roof is put on. The floor, or ceiling, can then be laid. The joists either can be set into the wall logs as shown in Figure 37 or the ends can project a foot or so as indicated by the dotted lines.

When building a cabin without a ceiling that is more than 15 ft., it may be advisable to lay one or more joists between the walls to prevent them from spreading in the midsection under the weight of the roof or snow.

CHINKING

Chinking is the process of filling up the open space between logs. It is necessary to exclude vermin and insects and to keep the cabin dry and comfortable. This is one of the most important operations in building a log cabin. The logs should be dry when chinking is done. Otherwise you will have a job of caulking or rechinking to do in a year or so due to the shrinkage of the logs. Logs and lumber, however, shrink only in diameter.

Chinking Material

In the Ozark Mountains mud or clay is commonly used for chinking. "Mud dauber" is the name applied to one who does this sort of work. Strips of wood are tacked in larger openings and the clay is worked to proper consistency and applied by hand. Thinner clay is later used to fill the cracks. Rain, of course, will wash out mud.

Sphagnum moss is sometimes used in the far north or wherever it is found. If not protected by chinking strips, however, it will dry up and will be pulled out by chipmunks; rats, and even birds.

Oakum is an excellent chinking material because it repells rats and bugs. It, too, requires reinforcement.

Plaster cement or mortar withstands weather better than anything else. A good mixture can be made of 3 parts Portland cement, 3 parts of clean washed sand, and 1 part of hydrated lime. It should be mixed so that it can be worked into cracks and small openings, and fill large openings without sagging. Several excellent prepared mortars are on the market. They are supplied in 100-lb. paper bags and require only mixing with water. Use an outside stucco plaster for the exterior and a wood mortar for the interior of the cabin. It is advisable to have a supply on hand, but it should be stored in a dry place. Incidentally, ready-mixed mortar is available for laying brick and stone also. It saves a lot of work.

Chinking is required whether the logs are set tight or whether there is space between them. In the case of the former, there may be a spline between the logs or the bottoms of the logs may be hollowed out to fit over the logs below. Both types of fitting require caulking. Oakum and in some places sphagnum moss, protected by some sort of wood or plaster shield, is used. Walls that are not solid require other methods. These are shown in Figure 38.

The simplest method of chinking is shown in Figure 38A. A thin sapling is nailed between the logs on the outside. Then sphagnum moss is driven between the logs from the inside and another sapling is nailed on the inside. These saplings may be peeled or not depending on the preference of the builder. Green saplings will form themselves to the surfaces to which they are nailed much better than dry ones. After drying out, however, they must be driven down tight again.

Figure 38B shows the same method with the exception that the saplings are cut into quarters. This makes a much neater job. This method and the above are common in the north where plaster is scarce. They are also employed if a fast job is in order.

Plaster is used for the chinking job shown in Figure 38C. Outside stucco plaster is very good for this purpose. Some builders drive a piece of metal lath between the logs and secure it with nails to anchor the plaster. For this purpose nails can also be driven into the logs as shown in the illustration. This method has been used with great success by the author.

Where there are large openings pieces of wood can be driven between the logs. These are nailed in place and plaster is spread over them. The plaster should be applied with a trowel and smoothed out in the form of a fillet with the hands. A pair of leather gloves will be found helpful.

Figure 38D shows a method employed in some sections of the Rocky Mountains. Instead of saplings, wedge-shaped strips cut out of 1-in. board as shown are driven between the logs and nailed in place on the inside of the cabin. If the wedges are wet they will fit over irregularities much better. Moss or oakum is forced between the logs from the outside. Next, a small, wedge-shaped strip of wood is nailed to each log on the outside as a retaining shelf for the fillet of plaster which is then applied.

The method last described is the neatest and most practical according to the writer's experience. The inside strips eliminate plaster, which fre-

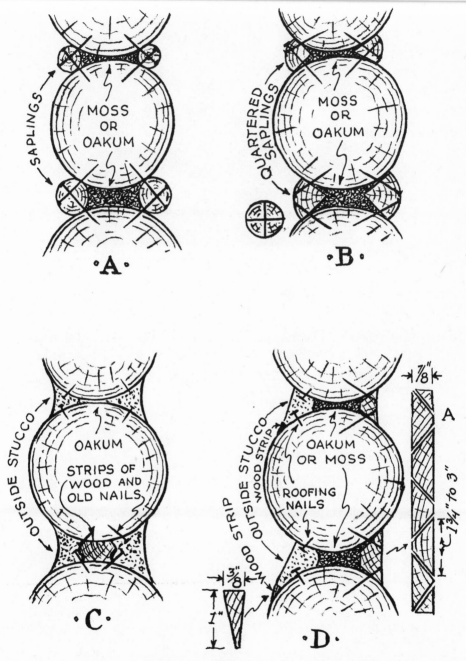

Fig. 38. Methods of chinking.

Drawknifing log before notching.

quently flakes off and causes needless dirt. The appearance of the interior will be greatly enhanced if the chinking strips are of the same wood as the logs. When the walls are oiled or waxed the wood will have a uniform color. The wedge-shaped strips on the outside make a substantial job because they prevent the plaster from feathering out and breaking off.

FINISHING THE LOGS

The inner walls should be as clean and bright as possible. Dark logs will produce a dark interior. Moreover, the logs should make an even-colored wall. With enough help the logs can be drawknifed on the inner surface as they are laid. First notch the log and fit it. Then roll it a quarter turn, that is, have the inner side uppermost; get someone to hold it steady, or wedge it; and shave off the inner surface. Then lay the log in position and spike it down. Thus the inside surface of your logs will be clean when laid up. To keep them in good condition put the roof on as soon as possible. Sun and rain will darken freshly shaved wood. Oil will not prevent discoloration if the logs are exposed too long to the weather.

To make a real job of it, the face of each chinking strip should be hand-planed with a slightly curved blade so that plane marks will show. There is no hurry about this, however, because the roof will be on when you are doing this work.

Some persons like to have the outside look like the inside. The logs, of course, will have to be drawknifed and later oiled and varnished. Individual preferences vary widely in this matter. I prefer an exterior with a natural weather color. I have seen some cabins painted brown with cream log ends, but I often wondered why the owner ever wanted a log cabin in the first place. Again I have seen entire interiors lathed and plastered. But these are extreme cases. A log cabin ceases to be a log cabin with such modifications. But the rustic beauty of the true log cabin appeals so much to the average person that no defense of it need be made here.

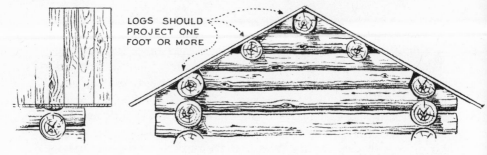

LOGS SHOULD
PROJECT ONE
FOOT OR MORE

Fig. 39.   Roof supported by horizontal members.

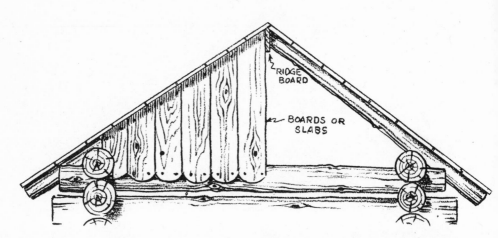

RIDGE
BOARD

BOARDS OR
SLABS

Fig. 40.   Roof supported by rafters.

Fig. 41.   Roof supported by special braces.

ROOFS

In planning the roof, the builder must consider its pitch and the projection of the eaves and the ridge. Practical advantages as well as artistic effect should be carefully weighed.

The roofs of log cabins as a rule do not have very much pitch. The average pitch or slope is about 5 in. to the foot. If it is much less than this, rain may drive in under the shingles.

Two common types of roof construction are shown in Figures 39 and 40. In Figure 39 the roof is supported by members running the length of the cabin. They are laid as the gable ends are built up and spiked at the ends. The small openings at the roof line are chinked later with plaster or wood or both.

The logs used for this purpose should be at least 8 in. in diameter especially in places that have heavy snowfalls. If the cabin is more than 12 or 14 ft. in length it may be necessary to build braces, like those in Figure 41, midway between the two end walls. If the room is very long such supports should be constructed about 8 to 10 ft. apart.

The roof boards run up and down with an overhang of 12 to 24 in. Before they are laid, a long, straight-edged board should be placed across the roof rafters to detect high spots. All of these should be leveled with a drawknife so that the roof boards can be set evenly in place. If wood shingles are to be used, the boards should be placed ¼ in. apart. This spacing will permit the shingles to dry both from the top and bottom. If composition material or tar paper is to be used for the roof, the boards should be laid close together, or better still, matched lumber is recommended.

Figure 40 shows the gable end of a roof supported by rafters. The

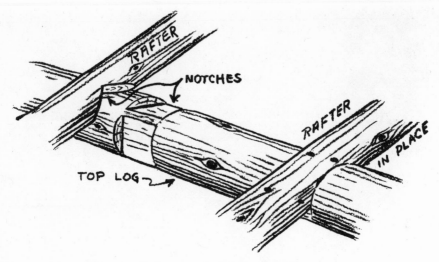

Fig. 42. Rafters notched into plate log.

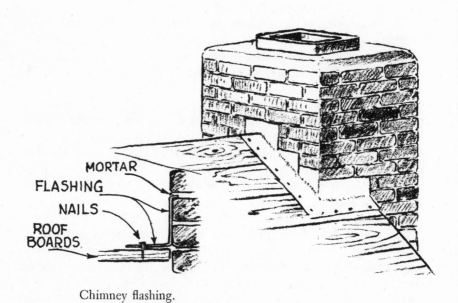

Chimney flashing.

Rafters laid.

logs used for the rafters should be about 6 in. at the butt. The rafters are set no more than 2 ft. apart. They are notched to the plate log as shown in Figure 42 and spiked. At the top the rafters are spiked to the ridge board. A 1-in. board will serve as a ridge board. The roof boards in this case run lengthwise. They, too, should be spaced ¼ to ½ in. apart if wood shingles are used, or closer together for composition or tar paper roofs.

Figure 40 also shows a method of closing up the gable ends. Wide boards or slabs can be used for this purpose. For weatherproofing they can be covered on the inside with a sheet of insulating board or heavy building paper or they may be backed with other boards running up and down. Battens can be nailed over the cracks if the cabin is only used for camping purposes.

FLASHING

Flashing is metal such as tin, copper, or galvanized sheet iron used to waterproof the roof where it meets the chimney, roof valleys (places where two roofs meet), etc. Chimney flashing is bent at right angles, tacked to the roof boards, and the upper edge of the portion which rests against the chimney is set into the mortar. The drawing at left shows how flashing is set into a brick chimney. The roofing material is laid over the flashing and the edges are sealed with roofing compound. If the flashing consists of more than one piece of metal, be sure to

49

allow sufficient overlap, or solder the joints. The laps can be sealed with roofing cement if no soldering equipment is available. Flashing usually is set into the mortar when the chimney is going up through the roof. If the chimney is built first, the mortar is chipped out where the flashing is to be set in. The edge of the flashing is then bent and set into the chimney and sealed with plaster. Chimney flashing should extend at least 4 in. beneath the shingles. Flashing for valleys should be at least 8 in. wide, which allows 4 in. for each side of the valley.

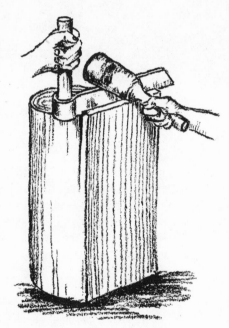

Fig. 43. Splitting shingles with a froe.

ROOFING MATERIAL

Most cabins have low-pitched roofs. This feature makes them picturesque but at the same time the job of rainproofing them is more difficult. Wood shingles on this type of roof have a tendency to leak. Hence, a good grade of composition roll or strip shingle roofing is recommended. This material is not only waterproof but is also very easy to apply. If the roof has a somewhat steep pitch, ordinary hand-split cedar or cypress shingles can be used. Figure 43 shows how shingles are split with a froe.

ROOF PATCHING

It is a good policy to have a can of roofing cement on hand. This is a thick asphalt preparation which can be applied with a putty knife or common table knife. It is excellent for repairing holes in roofing, sealing chimney flashing, caulking around windows, and so on. Once you use it you will wonder how the old-timers got along without it. Roofing cement also can be used to plug up mouse holes and to repair damage done by squirrels. They will not relish the taste of this material. And in inclement weather if you observe a bad spot in the chinking or chimney flashing you can make a good temporary repair by plugging it up with oakum and applying a coat of this cement.

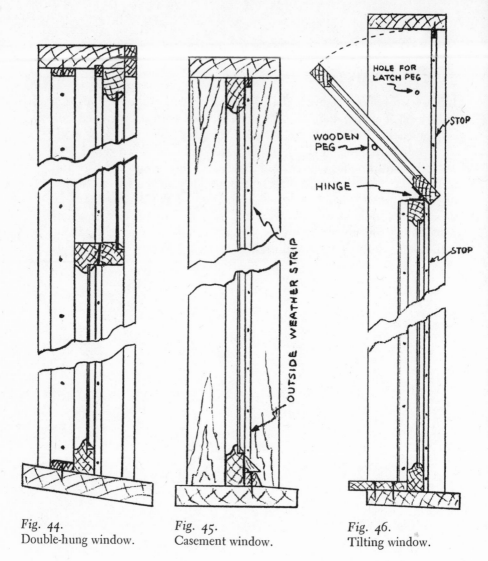

Fig. 44.
Double-hung window.

Fig. 45.
Casement window.

Fig. 46.
Tilting window.

Fig. 47. Spring bolt for
double-hinge window.

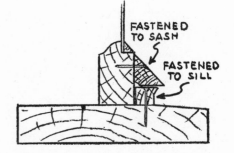

Fig. 48. Weather stripping for
casement window.

WINDOWS, DOORS, AND SHUTTERS

WINDOWS

There are three types of windows commonly used in log cabins which a layman can easily fit. They are regular double-hung windows, casement windows, and tilting windows. The double-hung window is illustrated in Figure 44. Note the 2-in. plank casing or frame. The upper and lower sash should fit together as indicated. The stops, however, need not be rabbeted into the frame but can be nailed. These windows have no weights; they are held open and locked shut with window springbolts like the one in Figure 47. Figure 34 shows how these windows appear from the outside. This type of window was used in the old log cabin built of square-hewn oak logs that was mentioned before and in the first section of the author's cabin.

Casement windows are more simple to install, but in my estimation they are not as weatherproof, unless one wishes to go to the expense and trouble of installing bronze weather stripping. Figure 45 is a sectional view of a casement window. Figure 48 shows how weather stripping can be applied at the bottom to keep out wind-driven rain at the sill. It should be noted that if these weather strips are too tight they will bind when wet, and if too loose they will leak. Casement windows swing inward and can be locked by means of ordinary casement-window latches. A good feature of casement windows is that they can be washed on both sides from the inside of the cabin.

The tilting window in Figure 46 is also rather simple to install. The upper section opens inward like a transom for ventilation while the lower sash is tight. Windows of this type are used in one of the sections of my cabin and are 40 in. wide.

I would like to say again at this time that log cabins as a rule are rather dark unless adequate fenestration is provided. If there is an exceptionally beautiful view from one or two sides of your cabin, it would be well to set in a large 6- or 8-ft. plate glass "picture window." Since these windows are large and heavy they will be stationary, so that ventilation will have to be supplied by means of doors and other windows. Picture windows, it is true, are not very rustic; in fact they are what might be termed ultra-modern. However, they can do much to brighten up a cabin. And with a picture window overlooking a mountain range, a lake, or river, or even a woodland view you can bring the great outdoors indoors. Be sure to have enough roof overhang to keep the window as clear as possible at all times.

DOORS

It has been pointed out already that one will find doors made of matched fencing lumber in some of the old log cabins that date back sixty or more years. Doors of this construction are still in existence. While they were not particularly strong, they served their purpose. Today they are used frequently as inside doors. Wainscot lumber also makes good inside doors.

Perhaps the best doors for log cabins are those made of 1¼- or 1½-in. dressed pine planks. Figure 49 shows a door made of such lumber with tongue-and-groove construction. Battens hold the planks together. Tongues and grooves are cut with a dado or with a special plane. Ready-made doors of this type can be ordered from a millwork company. Splines also can be used as in Figure 50. The doors shown in the photograph on page 65 were of this construction. The planks may be from 6 to 10 in. wide. These drawings show the inside of the doors. For battens 2 by 4-in. board is used, which usually measures 1½ by 3½ in. when dressed. They are fastened to the boards with 2½-in. lag screws, large wood screws, or large, square, iron cut nails. Lead holes should be drilled first irrespective of the method used and the planks should be clamped together while being fastened. The edges of each plank can be given a ¼ in. chamfer.

Very fine doors can be made of 1¼ by 3½-in. fir porch flooring. This material is tongued and grooved. If only ¾-in. lumber is on hand, a good outside door can be made similar to the batten door, described above, except that the top and bottom battens are flush with the top and bottom edges of the door. Three-inch batten strips are nailed along the two sides flush with the edges and two 2-in. battens are crossed from corner to corner. Then the side reinforced with battens is covered with ¾-in. lumber making a solid-looking door 1¼ in. thick.

Slabs make even a more picturesque door. The method of construction is the same. They are peeled and drawknifed evenly so that they all have the same general appearance. The battens are fastened on the flat side. If no tongues and grooves are cut, the cracks are sealed by means of ¼ by 1¼-in. batten strips.

Perhaps you prefer Dutch doors like those which are shown on page 56. The upper section may or may not have a window as desired. This is a very functional door. The top half can be opened for ventilation and the lower half can be left latched. Latches should be installed on both lower and upper sections of an outside Dutch door. There should also be a bolt latch to fasten the upper to the lower half. Cross battens should slant from the lower hinge edge to the upper latch edge as shown in the drawings. They keep the door from sagging.

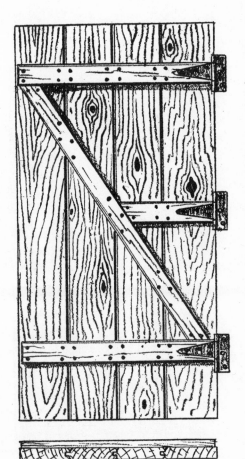

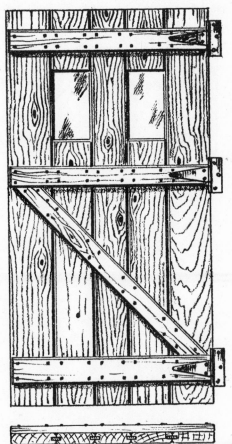

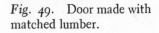

Fig. 49. Door made with matched lumber.

Fig. 50. Door made with splines.

Dutch doors.

SHUTTERS

The northern trapper used to leave his latch string out so that anyone in need of shelter would have access to his cabin. His place was locked, or rather latched, only against marauding animals. But in the highly civilized world today it is unwise to let a cabin stand in the woods without some sort of protection. As a rule some neighbors will keep an eye on it when it is not occupied. Nevertheless, ordinary precautions should be taken to safeguard your home. The doors should have good Yale locks in addition to latches. The windows require adequate protection. Even window screens are of some help, not much to be sure, but a little. A cabin that is not used during the fall and winter should be shuttered. The shutters can be made of 1-in. boards. They can either be hinged or secured with common wing fasteners like screens and storm windows. In either case they should be flush with the window frame, that is, set into the frames and fastened with hooks on the inside. It is not as easy to pry off a flush shutter as it is to pull off one that projects beyond the window frame. There are those who will say that if one wishes to break into a place there is nothing that will stop them. True, but remember, a boarded up home is not as inviting as a cozy little den with shades up and interior neatly appointed. And if a home is a little difficult to enter the thief or vandal will hesitate before trying.

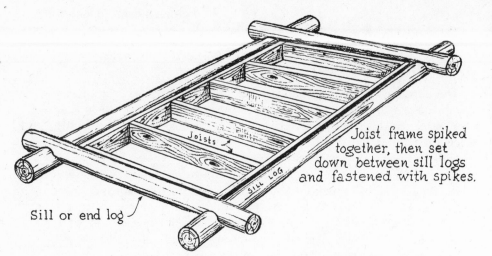

Joist frame spiked
together, then set
down between sill logs
and fastened with spikes.

Sill or end log

Fig. 51. Method of setting floor joists before walls are built.

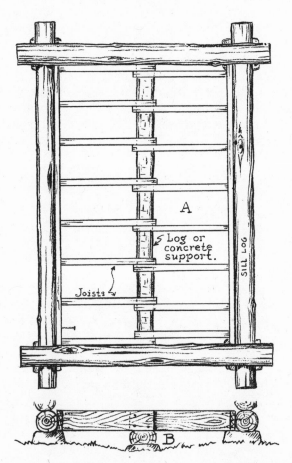

A

Log or
concrete
support.

Joists

SILL LOG

B

Fig. 52. Method of setting joists after walls and roof are up.

FLOORS, STAIRS, AND CEILINGS

FLOOR JOISTS

With the sills set and the corner joints squared, the floor joists can be laid. However, you may prefer to proceed immediately with the walls and then the roof. If you decide to put in the joists before the walls are laid, the method shown in Figure 51 should be followed. It is quite simple. Take two 2 by 10-in. planks and nail them temporarily to the sill logs. Then lay out the points at which the joists are to be located. Measure the length of each joist separately and carefully cut them to these lengths. Next remove the planks from the sill logs and spike the joists between them, each in its proper place. Forty-penny spikes should be used for this purpose. Now set the assembled joists in place between the sills. This frame should fit tightly. Level off the frame and fasten the assembly to the sills with 40-penny spikes.

If the floor joists are laid after the walls and roof are built the method illustrated in Figure 52 is recommended. At A it can be seen that the framework is divided into two sections. This construction facilitates spiking the ends of the joists to the long members in the restricted working area provided by the interior of the cabin. One is fastened with spikes to the right-hand sill log, the other to the left-hand sill. The joists are supported at the center upon a log or concrete support running down the middle of the cabin as shown at B. The ends of the joists should be spiked together where they meet at the center. It goes without saying that any irregularities or bumps on the sill logs must be carefully leveled off as the carrying power of the floor depends upon

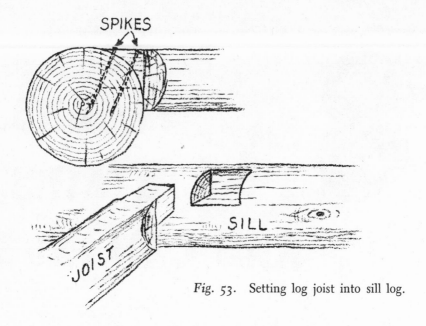

SPIKES

JOIST

SILL

Fig. 53. Setting log joist into sill log.

how well the side planks and sills are fastened together. Joists should be spaced about 16 in. to centers.

If you are building your cabin in true backwoods style, you will use logs for floor joists. The sill logs are notched and the joists set in the notches as shown in Figure 53. Now the tops of the logs must be leveled so that the floor will be level. Since logs differ in dimensions, it would be best to lay the joists and spike them in place before hewing off. A long straight board and a level will have to be used for this purpose. If 2-in. plank flooring or a double floor is laid, the joists can be located from 18 to 24 in. apart. A 12-ft. span or more requires a supporting sill through the center as shown in Figure 52.

FLOORS

The floors should not be laid until the cabin has been chinked and the windows and doors hung. Since it is very unlikely that your cabin will have a basement, special care should be taken to build a floor that will be dry and sturdy. The ultimate in economy for a small summer cabin is a floor of 3-in., matched, yellow pine. This can be stained and waxed with excellent results. A good grade of fir porch flooring would be still better and more serviceable. An ideal type of floor construction is shown in Figure 54. Laid first is a subfloor of matched flooring of any kind or even 6-in. matched fencing. Over this a layer of good, tarred felt paper is placed. Then the floor of fir, yellow pine, or oak is laid with the boards running in the opposite direction of those of the sub-floor.

Perhaps you prefer a floor made of 2-in. planks. They should be tongued and grooved and for best appearance they should measure from 8 to 12 in. in width. To prevent warping due to dampness, the bottom and edges of the planks should be oiled before they are laid and they should be fastened with heavy screws. This, of course, means work but it will be well worth the effort. For the screws, first drill a hole halfway through the plank slightly larger than the head to provide ample room for the screwdriver to turn. Then drill a lead hole slightly larger than the shank. The planks will pull down tightly. Plug the holes with dowels and cut them off flush. All the floor boards must be even before finishing is begun.

Figure 55 shows how mopboards and quarter-round molding are set around the floor.

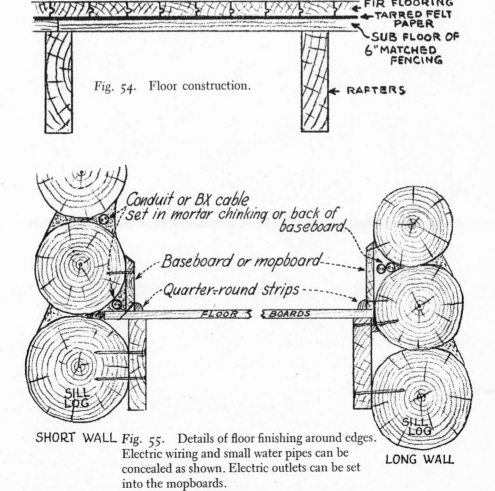

Fig. 54. Floor construction.

FIR FLOORING
TARRED FELT PAPER
SUB FLOOR OF 6"MATCHED FENCING
RAFTERS

Conduit or BX cable set in mortar chinking or back of baseboard
Baseboard or mopboard
Quarter-round strips
FLOOR BOARDS
SILL LOG
SILL LOG

SHORT WALL Fig. 55. Details of floor finishing around edges. Electric wiring and small water pipes can be concealed as shown. Electric outlets can be set into the mopboards.

LONG WALL

FINISHING

A good preparation for finishing a cabin is a mixture of 1 part turpentine and 3 parts boiled linseed oil to which is added a small amount of maple or walnut oil stain. It is applied liberally with a brush and after being allowed to soak for a while it is wiped off. When the first coat has dried, another thin coat is put on and permitted to dry. The floor then is given a coat or two of nonrubbing wax. If this is done about twice a year the floor will be kept in good condition. Do not varnish cabin floors and walls. If you must varnish the walls, use a flat varnish.

The same 3 to 1 mixture can be used for logs, windows, sashes, and frames. All woodwork, of course, must be cleaned before oiling. Incidentally the floor will look better if it is slightly darker than the rest of the woodwork. You can, of course, use your judgment in this matter.

Fig. 56. A single stairs made with a half log for a stringer and slots for treads.

A well-insulated ceiling sealed along the edges.

STAIRS

If you need a stairway for access to a second floor or a loft, it should be made of the same material as the rest of the cabin. Slabs or half logs can be used as shown in Figure 56. It may be necessary to build the stairs steeper than shown here and perhaps a sapling rail may be required. The back of the stairway can be closed up and cupboards can be built beneath it.

CEILINGS

In the small cabin a ceiling usually can be dispensed with, the roof itself forming the ceiling. If the cabin is to be used in winter, the roof should be insulated with any one of the good insulating wallboards. This can be cut to fit between the rafters or nailed over the rafters to form an air space. Painted a light color, such a ceiling will brighten the room or rooms immensely.

If the ceiling is of matched lumber, for additional insulation, insulating board can be nailed against the ceiling between the joists. This will pay good dividends in cold weather and will add to your comfort during hot weather. The photograph below illustrates this treatment.

Instead of laying a double floor as is usually the case in frame houses, insulating board can be nailed between the rafters as shown in Figure 57. The photograph on page 63 shows a ceiling of insulating board in one part of my cabin. The roof was made of old lumber with heavy asphalt building paper for insulation and heavy, slate-covered, asphalt strip shingles. This was not sufficient to hold the heat in the wintertime, so a ceiling was built as shown in the photograph. It was made of ¾-in. celotex and to gain height it was laid up against the rafters to a distance of 4 ft.

The insulating board is nailed to a ceiling of matched fencing. Note the wide battens.

6" matched fencing
¾" insulating board

Batten strips

Insulating board must be
bent slightly to get it up in
place, unless rafters are half logs

Fig. 57. Ceiling construction.

If you like icicles, don't insulate your ceiling
and roof.

 PARTITIONS,
ADDITIONS,
AND PORCHES

PARTITIONS

If there are to be log partitions or additional rooms in the form of wings, all walls are put up at the same time. Of course, if lumber or plaster is to be used, the procedure will be different. In the latter case the partitions would be built later.

Partitions can be notched as shown in Figure 58 or the logs may project as they do at the corners. Projecting ends are sometimes more picturesque. If the ends of the logs are chopped and staggered at the corners, the ends of partition logs should also be prepared in this manner. When building out a wing, it is best to dovetail the inside corners.

At this point I would like to insert an important note about partitions in larger cabins. Logs at their very best do not reflect much light. It is advisable, therefore, that you attempt to compensate for their poor light-reflecting qualities. Now a light-colored plaster partition in a cabin will reflect the light from the windows and will brighten an otherwise dark room considerably. Such a wall will not detract from the appearance of rustic simplicity that you have in mind. The cabin shown in the photograph on page 8 had a plastered wall partition. This cabin, incidentally, was built in southern Wisconsin when Indians were still to be seen about the countryside. It was made of square-hewn logs with dovetail corners. The roof, which was covered with white-oak shakes, was doing good service as late as 1918. A band of Seneca Indians on the way from Green Bay to Muskego lakes stopped to watch the men who were doing the shingling. The doors of the cabin were of 2 by 6-in. matched fencing with battens on the inside.

ADDITIONS

If you have only one or two helpers, you will have more than enough work to build a one-room cabin during a single vacation season. You can always enlarge it. Even if your needs call for a more elaborate structure, it might be a good idea not to try to do the entire job in one fell swoop. In this way you will certainly enjoy the work much more and you will very likely do a better job.

For additions, of course, piers, or, if you desire them, foundation walls or a basement are required. They are constructed in the same manner as described previously.

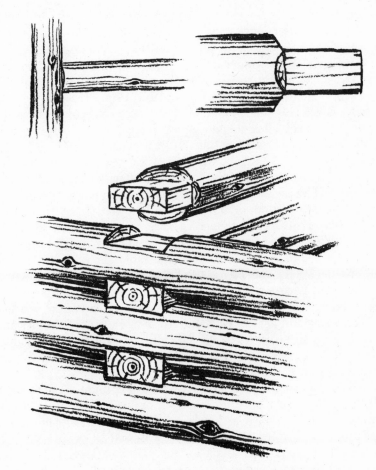

Fig. 58. Notching logs for partitions or additions.

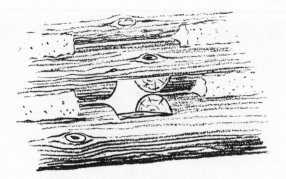

Fig. 59. Mortise cut for partition.

Joining the addition to the cabin proper requires a little ingenuity at times. The neatest method is to tie the logs into the walls of the cabin, provided they are of the same diameter as the original ones, as shown in Figure 58. First the chinking is removed and then the mortise is cut. The upper half of the opening between the logs can be chiseled out and then the lower half can be sawed and completed with a chisel (Fig. 59). When chiseling, be careful not to loosen the chinking plaster. If the logs are small, all of the sawing can be done with a large keyhole saw. The use of this tool takes time but it is efficient.

A simpler method is to shape the ends of the new logs to conform to the sides of the old logs and fasten them with long lag screws as shown in Figure 61. These fasteners are rather scarce because they are seldom used and therefore are not often stocked in hardware stores. If you cannot buy screws of sufficient length, have a blacksmith weld pieces from 4 to 6 in. long to regular 6-in. lag screws (Fig. 60). To fasten the cedar logs to the old tamarack logs of the cabin shown in the photograph (page 70, left) and Figure 62, I had to elongate the lag screws in this manner. Each log is fastened as it is laid up. A loose-fitting hole is bored through the old log and a pilot hole into the end of the new log. The holes in the old log can be countersunk to allow for a washer and the head of the lag screw. Then they are plugged with plastic wood and no one will be the wiser. The ends of the new logs can be shaped to fit with an ax or saw. The latter is much faster.

When the logs are of a different size, you will encounter a little more difficulty in obtaining a good fit. However, results will be satisfactory if the work is done as shown in Figure 62. Plaster will take care of any irregularities. As pointed out elsewhere, it is well to drive a few old nails across the larger gaps to anchor the plaster or mortar. However, drive in the nails far enough so that they will be covered.

ADDED SECTION

Fig. 60. Lag screw elongated by welding.

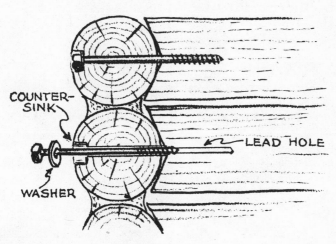

COUNTER-
SINK

WASHER

LEAD HOLE

Fig. 61. New logs fastened to wall
of same size logs.

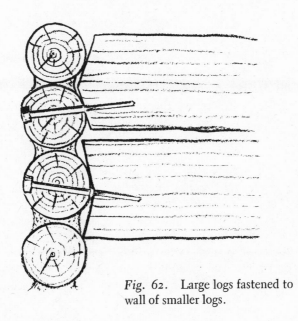

Fig. 62. Large logs fastened to
wall of smaller logs.

Left: Corner with new logs joining old logs.
Right: Door at junction of old section and addition.

It is not unlikely that you will need an outside door in the addition. It can be made as explained elsewhere, but it may be to your advantage to construct the door as shown in Figure 63. The ends of logs of the original unit are sawed off straight and one side of the door frame is set against them. Notice how the sill log is spliced to the old sill log. This method was used for an addition to my cabin. The sketch shows the details and the photograph above right shows how it looked when finished.

It might be mentioned here that all the tricks and short cuts possible in log-cabin construction could not be numbered, much less described and illustrated. Hence, this work will provide ample opportunity to display your resourcefulness. I am showing some typical problems and am explaining how they were solved. With a little ingenuity and common sense any obstacle can be surmounted. Often some difficulty will call for much thought and will entail a great deal of argumentation, but then that is half the fun of building a log cabin.

LEAN-TOS

A lean-to is commonly used as a kitchen, woodshed, tool or work shed, or even a bedroom. It can be built of rough-sawed lumber or slabs and can be made to harmonize with the cabin proper. The boards should be of different widths to look interesting. Batten strips, 1½ in. wide, can be nailed on the outside over the cracks. If matched lumber is used, the outside can be covered with cedar shingles. I used old barn boards for a small kitchen lean-to, but to keep out the cold in winter I covered it with a layer of building paper and shingles. The boards on such an addition should run up and down and the board next to the log wall must be cut out (Fig. 64).

Fig. 63. Door frame of new section set against log ends of first section.

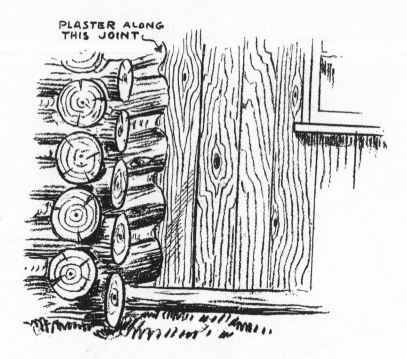

Fig. 64. Boards of lean-to cut to fit logs.

Lean-to made of logs.

PORCHES

Porches are designed and built for a number of purposes, some of them entirely practical, others less so. As a general rule they are constructed to protect the doorway from rain and snow, or to provide a dry storage place for firewood. They are made larger to provide an outside, partially sheltered place for lunches and meals. Elaborate, screened porches are

Rafters toe-nailed to top log

Fig. 65. Simple porch construction.

73

sometimes seen, but they more properly belong to the discussion of additions.

The photograph on page 13 shows a porch built several years ago of tamarack saplings which were plentiful at the time. This has been replaced by a new one made of cedar logs, very plain, as you can see by the photograph below, but much more substantial.

It is best to set rafters for porch roofs up and down, running parallel with the cabin (Fig. 65). The roof itself will very likely have little pitch. Hence it should be covered with a good grade of tar paper and cement rather than shingles. No rain will drive underneath this.

Porch.

FIXTURES & FIREPLACE EQUIPMENT

After the essentials of your cabin have been taken care of and the hard work is over, you will probably feel like coasting awhile. But you won't remain idle long. Soon you will have the urge to do something to make the place just a bit more pleasant and comfortable. From now on there will be a multitude of little things to be taken care of, but each job will be more fun than the previous one.

DOOR LATCHES AND LOCKS

Of course, you will have a good tumbler lock on each door. Although these locks are modern, they are very essential. But you can make latches of hardwood like those shown in Figures 66 and 67 that will be ornamental as well as useful. The one is a sliding latch and the other a lift latch. They are placed on the inside of the door and are operated from the outside by means of either a latch string or knob. A slot must be cut in the door for the knob. For the type of latch in Figure 66 the slot is horizontal; for the one in Figure 67 it is in the form of a short arc. The wedge hanging from the nail in Figure 67 is inserted in the opening of the vertical U piece above the latch to lock the door from the inside. This latch will also lock the door automatically if the catch is smooth. A piece of brass or tin tacked on the slope of the catch will allow the latch to slide easily.

Perhaps you like wrought-iron latches and hinges. These can be purchased at hardware stores that handle building materials. The common fault, however, that I find in wrought-iron trimmings is that they are too elaborate. Remember, the pioneers had very little time and less

Fig. 66.   Sliding latch.   *Fig.* 67.   Lifting latch.

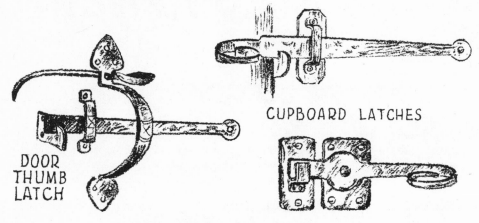

CUPBOARD LATCHES

DOOR
THUMB
LATCH

Fig. 68.   Wrought-iron latches.

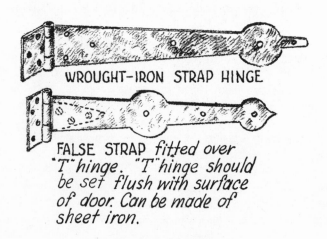

WROUGHT-IRON STRAP HINGE

FALSE STRAP *fitted over*
"T" hinge. "T" hinge should
be set flush with surface
of door. Can be made of
sheet iron.

Fig. 69.   Wrought-iron hinges.

iron. They made their hardware sturdy and simple. Wrought-iron latches (Fig. 68) can be beautiful in their simplicity and will last as long as your log cabin.

HINGES

Hinges can be forged out of heavy sheet iron or strap iron if you like to do such work. A small portable forge and anvil are very practical additions to your list of building equipment. The straps also can be cut out of sheet iron with a cold chisel and a few hammer marks can be made for effect. The straps can be put on after the ordinary hinges as shown in Figure 69.

DOOR AND CUPBOARD HANDLES

Handles for doors and cupboards also should be of a rustic type. Oddly shaped pieces with a natural curve are often used. Odd growths usable for this purpose can be found in the woods without too much difficulty if one is on the lookout for them. Deer and elk horn also make fine door handles (Fig. 70).

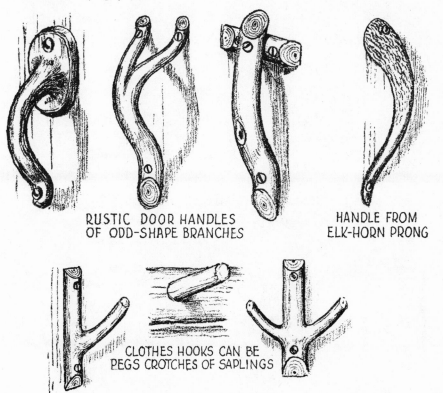

RUSTIC DOOR HANDLES
OF ODD-SHAPE BRANCHES

HANDLE FROM
ELK-HORN PRONG

CLOTHES HOOKS CAN BE
PEGS CROTCHES OF SAPLINGS

Fig. 70. Door and cupboard handles.

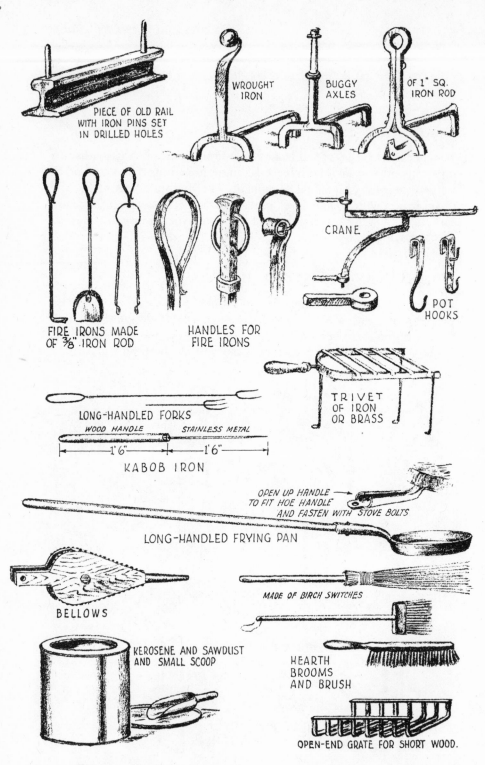

PIECE OF OLD RAIL WITH IRON PINS SET IN DRILLED HOLES

WROUGHT IRON

BUGGY AXLES

OF 1" SQ. IRON ROD

CRANE

POT HOOKS

FIRE IRONS MADE OF ⅜" IRON ROD

HANDLES FOR FIRE IRONS

TRIVET OF IRON OR BRASS

LONG-HANDLED FORKS

WOOD HANDLE   STAINLESS METAL

1' 6"   1' 6"

KABOB IRON

OPEN UP HANDLE TO FIT HOE HANDLE AND FASTEN WITH STOVE BOLTS

LONG-HANDLED FRYING PAN

BELLOWS

MADE OF BIRCH SWITCHES

KEROSENE AND SAWDUST AND SMALL SCOOP

HEARTH BROOMS AND BRUSH

OPEN-END GRATE FOR SHORT WOOD.

Fig. 71. Fireplace equipment.

FIREPLACE EQUIPMENT

The early pioneers did all of their cooking over an open fire. From their fireplace equipment you can get many ideas for appointing your hearth and fireplace in a very effective manner.

Starting with andirons, you have a large choice ranging from two pieces of rail to wrought-iron firedogs (Fig. 71). The last mentioned need not be fancy, highly polished pieces of modern design; they should be the type that a country blacksmith could make out of old wagon tires.

Of equal importance is a set of fire irons. This set will include first of all a good poker with a hook on it for turning logs. Next you will need a pair of tongs to pick up hot coals and burning fragments that fall off of the andirons. The third piece will be a shovel for removing the ashes.

From the crane shown in the illustration you can suspend an iron kettle and perhaps two or three pot hooks of different lengths. You might also try to find a couple of iron kettles for atmosphere.

If you are going to use your fireplace for cooking, and I know that you eventually will, there is nothing so handy as a long-handled frying pan and a long-handled broiler. There are two of each in my cabin and we would not know how to prepare a fireplace meal without them. Broilers of this kind can be purchased, but the frying-pan handle you will have to supply yourself. I once used an old hoe handle for an exceptionally large pan. Make the handle long enough, at least 4 ft., and 5 ft. is even better. It can be fastened by means of stove bolts or rivets. But don't try to fasten a long handle to a cast-iron pan. Use a stamped sheet-iron pan for this purpose. It will be a real pleasure to use this over an open fire both indoors and outdoors.

A trivet will be found very handy when cooking over an open grate. Dishes or a frying pan can be set on it.

Then make a dozen long-handled forks for roasting weiners. You may prefer kabob sticks like the one shown in the drawing. Green willow sticks can be used, but there is no danger that the metal type will burn.

Bellows are both decorative and useful. And while I am on the subject, I would like to say that the best fire starter that I know of is sawdust soaked with kerosene. It should be stored in a tight can. A handful of this material with some small wood placed over it will get a fire going in short order. This is not a genuine backwoods method of starting a fire, I suppose, but no one will complain about it when the results are seen, especially the one delegated to do the job on a cold morning.

A wood basket I hardly need mention. You will soon learn that one is very essential. You can either buy or make it yourself without great difficulty.

Two more important items should be mentioned. One is a fireplace screen. A good fire of oak, ash, or maple will seldom throw sparks into the room, but softwoods such as pine, hemlock, poplar, and basswood will. Therefore a wire screen that will cover the entire opening of the fireplace is essential. You will also find a brush or broom a handy article to have leaning against the fireplace.

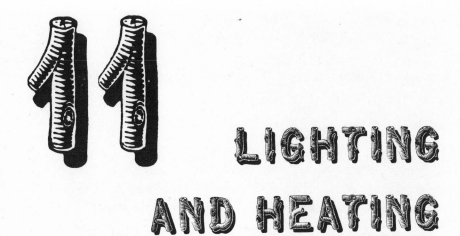

11 LIGHTING AND HEATING

LIGHTING

In my cabin I ran the gamut of lighting from candles to electric fixtures. We had to install electricity for practical reasons in spite of the coziness of candle and lamp light, which is used now only for very special occasions. A word about the history of my cabin will give a good picture of the evolution of lighting systems in such a dwelling.

My home is located on the outskirts of a small town on a plot of land that extends from a main highway several hundred feet to a brook. Toward the rear the property is rather heavily wooded and it is here that the log cabin was erected, for building in the northwoods or elsewhere at that time was not possible as far as I was concerned. The cabin was intended primarily for use as a work and tool house. There were benches for woodwork and iron work and in one corner a forge and anvil (see the photograph on page 82). Heat was supplied only by the fireplace. It was a swell place for friendly gatherings and we thoroughly enjoyed working there, making wrought-iron fixtures, rustic furniture, and so on. One gasoline lantern was used, to which we added a large tin reflecting shade to throw the light down on the work. It provided more than enough illumination except when it ran out of gasoline and this occurred usually when the light was needed most.

We then decided to convert the cabin into a gift shop. Some remodeling was required. A center partition of knotty pine was put in. Shelves were built on the partition and along the walls. We discovered that in order to display lighting fixtures and wrought-iron and other semirustic

Author at forge and anvil used for wrought-iron work.

lamps the cabin would have to be wired. BX cable was used for this purpose and was run between the logs as shown in Figure 55.

The gift shop was a success, but the family decided to use the cabin as sort of a summer home. We lived in it for a few weeks every spring while our garden was being prepared and planted. It was fun. During the evenings I made rustic lamps and fixtures to dress up the cabin. These lamps, of course, were electrified and the wiring was concealed. They provided adequate light for reading and working.

Recently my cabin has been converted into a combination museum and workshop. It has been enlarged and remodeled. The rooms have ivory celotex ceilings. There are two flush lights in the ceiling of the larger room and four Indian katcina lamps on the walls. This arrangement provides a much better distribution of light than the old gasoline lamp, not to mention a more pleasant atmosphere. Now we have light whenever and wherever we need it. Candlelight we use on occasion and often we do without light entirely and sit before a bright, crackling fire of cedar or poplar logs and go back a hundred years.

Unless you are going modern, there will be no wide concrete walks around your cabin and leading to it. It is more than likely that you will have flagstone or gravel walks. While these can be made very firm they are never as smooth as concrete. Then, too, the nights will be dark and there will be many trees around and about—hence the need for good porch and yard light. You can make the fixtures yourself, but be sure that they illuminate the grounds and do not blind. Rustic lamps strategically placed are therefore very practical and will enhance the beauty of your place.

In planning your lights and lighting system you will have a fine opportunity to express your individuality. It is hardly possible to make specific recommendations that would be equally acceptable to the varying tastes of individual builders. In my cabin the Indian motif is pronounced. The walls are decorated with Indian clothing, pipes, tom-toms, and eagle feathers. Whatever you do, keep your cabin rustic.

HEATING

I suppose that when everything is said and done, adequate heating is the most important requirement in a cabin that is to be used in cold weather. In moderate temperature, a fireplace is able to keep a cabin comfortably warm. But a fireplace alone will not suffice in severe cold unless it is of the sheet-iron type, which has been discussed already. An ideal combination is a fireplace and some kind of stove. Thus the stove will supply ample heat and the fireplace will draw the cold air from the floor and carry it up the chimney. The latter, of course, will throw out a good amount of heat, especially after it has been in operation for about two hours and the stones and bricks are heated through.

For efficiency, economy, and atmosphere, the combination stove shown in the photograph to the left on this page cannot be surpassed. It burns wood and coal. A fire can be kept going for about twelve

Coal and wood stove.

Wood-burning stove made
of 50-gallon oil drum.

hours and the room will stay warm. It will operate at about a quarter of the cost of an oil stove.

The other stove shown above was made from a 40-gal. oil drum. Firebricks 1 in. thick were laid on the bottom of the drum and part way up the sides to retain the heat. Such a stove can be made easily by anyone who is handy with tools. This quick-heating stove will warm a 16 by 28-ft. room within an hour during subzero weather. A fire can be kept going in it overnight if a couple of green chunks of wood are tossed into it on retiring. Coal cannot be used because there is no grate.

Of course, other types of wood stoves will also serve well in cold weather. For example there is the wood-burning cooking and baking oven which was common a few years back. A sheet-iron stove like the one in Figure 72 is quick-heating, but like all wood stoves it requires constant attention. However, in the experience of the author, the combination wood and coal stove discussed above will supply ample heat at all times with a minimum of attention and will add rather than detract from the appearance of the cabin.

Some people may prefer an oil stove, with which the author also has experimented. An oil stove, however, will not harmonize with the rest of the interior of the cabin as well as a good wood stove.

Fig. 72. Airtight stove.

12 RE-CONDITIONING OLD LOG CABINS

If you have come into possession of an old log cabin or if your own cabin is in need of repair, you probably will like a few suggestions for reconditioning it. The typical city home can be fixed readily with paint or wallpaper or both. A log cabin, however, is different in this respect and may require improvements that are a bit more difficult to make.

One of the most common defects in old cabins is loose chinking. This, of course, must be removed completely and a little trouble will be encountered at times.

Next, the logs must be cleaned. If they are peeled, they will have become darkened with age and will need scraping. The logs can be shaved with an ordinary short-handled floor scraper, provided they are smooth, that is, without too many knots. There are several different types of floor scrapers on the market (Fig. 73); the type of scraper used by cabinet-makers will also work. Some have reversible blades, and others, double blades. A long-handled scraper, however, is the best. These tools must be sharp and must be kept in that condition for satisfactory results. After the loose chinking has been removed, the logs can readily be prepared to look new and fresh without too much difficulty.

If the bark is still on the logs the problem is altogether different. Now the first unit of my cabin was made of unpeeled tamarack. Only the loose outer bark had been scraped off. The logs looked truly excellent at the time. The reddish browns and purples gave the walls a beautiful color. Soon, however, large black ants and other borers began to inhabit our elegant walls and eventually the bark had to be removed.

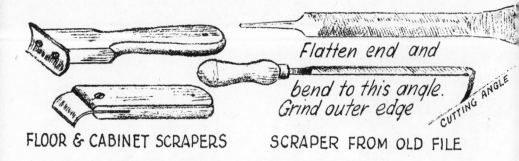

FLOOR & CABINET SCRAPERS

Flatten end and
bend to this angle.
Grind outer edge

CUTTING ANGLE

SCRAPER FROM OLD FILE

Fig. 73. Scrapers.

For this I made scrapers of old files about 1½ in. wide. The ends were heated and flattened to a sharp edge and then bent as shown in Figure 73. With a scraper of this kind and a good pair of arms and wrists, in one motion you can remove bark and from ¼ to ⅜ in. of sapwood in which the bugs like to bore. If the tool is held at the correct angle, a cutting action can be effected which will produce a much smoother finish than scraping, but the scraper must be sharpened every so often.

After the bark has been removed, brush off the dust and rechink as necessary. For applying the mortar, use a small trowel and a hawk, as shown in Figure 74. I used a small molders' tool employed for finishing sand molds and have not found anything superior to it for a partially

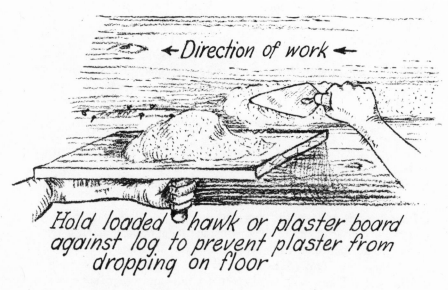

←Direction of work ←

Hold loaded hawk or plaster board
against log to prevent plaster from
dropping on floor

Fig. 74. Small trowel and hawk used for applying mortar.

Removing bark with bent-file scraper.

Old walls scraped and replastered.

chinked wall. When a section of about 3 ft. is completed, go over the plaster with a 4-in. wet paint brush. For this operation a brush was kept on hand in a pan of water. Both old and new plaster was given this treatment with the result that you see in the photograph (page 87, bottom). Trowel marks are effective in new chinking but not for patches in old mortar.

If the logs have been scraped clean, they need only be oiled. The walls will be very light and will look like new. The outside walls can also be scraped and rechinked but need not be oiled.

FLOORS

If old floors are not too badly worn, they can be sanded with a power floor sander. A machine of this type can be rented. As a rule, however, it is better to lay new flooring crosswise. To lay linoleum over a rough floor is a waste of time and money.

CEILINGS

For a new ceiling any one of the many different kinds of insulating board can be nailed over the old one. On the other hand, it may be necessary to put up an entirely new ceiling. The openings can be filled with wood mortar where the insulating board meets the logs, and large battens can be used to cover the joints between the sections.

13 OUTDOOR FIREPLACES

Though the interior of your cabin may be beautiful and comfortable, there will be many times during the summer months that you will want to eat outdoors, the mosquitoes permitting. It is more than likely, therefore, that you will want some kind of outdoor fireplace on your grounds. Everyone who cooks outdoors has his pet theory concerning outdoor fireplaces. Let us consider a few types here and you can then determine which one will suit your needs best.

The first question that I ask a person desiring information on outdoor fireplaces is: For what purpose are you going to use it? Possibly you want it to roast weiners or to prepare hamburgers, steaks, corn, or bean-hole beans. There are those, too, who like to prepare an entire meal on an outdoor fireplace. A few points, therefore, should be taken into consideration before you build. A little planning will be well worth the satisfaction of having a well-constructed and efficient fireplace. Of course, if you are a camp cook and a master of all of the tricks of camp cooking, and in addition don't mind blackened pots and pans, you may not even need a fireplace.

During the past few years, very beautiful outdoor fireplaces of the chimney type have been built both in parks and on private grounds. The typical fireplace of this kind is made of the same stone used for the house, has pleasing proportions, and is located at some choice point on the property. Chimney fireplaces are rarely passed without being noticed and admired. However, you probably will not be looking for something quite so elaborate, and they do have one drawback. The outside of the chimney nearest the fire is inclined to become blacker than the flue. Why? I'll answer this question with a question. Why should the smoke seek its way over to the chimney when there is nothing to prevent it from rising directly upward? Smoke simply will follow the line of least resistance. Thus these chimneys are ornamental rather than functional. Logically, if you wanted the chimney to work you would be required to build an outdoor stove. If smoke is to go up a chimney, every other outlet must be closed. All of this, however, is still no argument against the beauty of the chimney fireplace. Here, however, we will limit ourselves to a few basic designs of the simpler type of outdoor fireplace. I trust that my experience with them will help you in planning and building one that will have all of the features you will want.

A.   Sectional view.

B.   Perspective view.

Fig. 75.   Pit fireplace.

MATERIALS

The principles governing the selection of materials for outdoor fireplaces are the same as those for indoor fireplaces. You will recall that in our discussion of the latter, you were warned about the danger of exploding stones. It was explained that while some stones will react favorably to heat, some will not; hence the advisability of using firebrick for the firepot. While my present outdoor fireplace has caused no difficulty in this regard, let me tell you of my experience with one that did. A few years ago I made a very fine fireplace in northern Michigan, where we had to do all our cooking outdoors. Fortunately I did not go to the trouble of using mortar but merely saw to it that the stones were laid up symmetrically and firmly. We then went about the not too unpleasant task of preparing our first meal. A fire was started and everything was coming along very well until the stones started to explode. It's a good joke now but then it was far from funny. We ate a cold meal that night. I have seen this same thing happen many times since and am always skeptical, therefore, when using stone in a strange locality. To play safe, line your outdoor fireplace with firebrick just as you did with the fireplace in your cabin. You will note that firebrick is shown in each drawing. I used it in my fireplace not only to insure myself against the possibility of having to build another one but also because they are easier to work with. The facing that you see in the photographs is cut limestone. Any field stone can be used around the outside, for only the firebrick lining will have to withstand very intense heat. You can also use common building brick for the exterior if no stones are available.

PIT FIREPLACE

The pit fireplace shown in Figure 75 is ideal for preparing bean-hole beans, roasted corn, and is very satisfactory for all other types of roasting, broiling, and frying. Built with a firebrick lining, it is easy to clean out with a rake or hoe. The ashes are simply pulled up the incline and disposed of. A shovel also can be used. Then, too, you can easily rake out the live embers to provide for a dutch oven on the hot firebrick and then shovel or push them back to cover the pot. Similarly in the pit fireplace, the embers easily can be raked right over the corn for roasting.

This fireplace has one drawback; it is rather low. On the other hand, a low fireplace is better for a camp fire than a high one. When you stop to think how people enjoy sitting around a fire at night after a good outdoor meal, a fireplace that will hold a fire is very desirable.

Figure 75A is a sectional view of a pit fireplace. The upright brick in

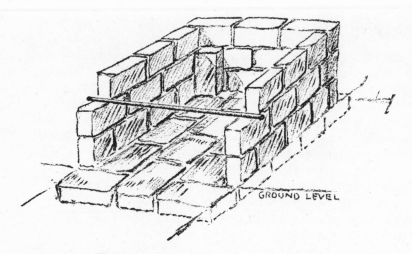

Fig. 76.   Surface fireplace.

Fig. 77.   Raised fireplace.

Surface fireplace.

the lower right corner is a support for the grate, the lower end of which rests on the ground in front. If this brick is set higher, you will have to use a brick in front so that the grate will be level, but then you will not have to raise the grate to put wood on the fire.

Figure 75B shows the pit fireplace in perspective. Here it can be seen clearly how the stone is mortared around the brick. At the left is a table of flat stone for pots and pans. If this is open, kindling wood can be stored here and, of course, a rather large stone will be required.

SURFACE FIREPLACE

The surface fireplace shown in Figure 76 will be found very satisfactory for general, all-round, outdoor cooking. You will notice that there are no projecting iron lugs such as are sometimes used to support the grates nor are there any other unnecessary fixtures. The floor is set flush with the ground. Stone of any kind should be mortared around, as brick set on end would not hold. Note the brick mortared in the corner. It is level with the projecting bricks in front. A loose iron rod will support the forward end of the grate and the corner bricks will

Reflector oven used in conjunction with
a surface fireplace.

hold the other end. If the rod is loose, it can be removed for cleaning
out the fireplace or starting fires.

As far as baking is concerned, with the reflector oven in the photograph on page 94 you can get some very fine results. With a good fire,
you can bake a pan of biscuits in about ten minutes in this oven. At
the same time you can roast corn or broil steaks on the fireplace proper.
This will hurry along the preparation of the meal. I used an old window
grate with bars about 1½ in. apart, which is just about right for sweet
corn in husks. The corn is soaked in water from four to eight hours
before roasting time. The ears are then laid on the grate close together,
and if the fire is at all brisk, you can keep the upper half of the ears
wet with a bundle of corn husks without putting out the fire. Then
after about fifteen minutes, depending on the heat, the ears are turned
and the green sides are roasted, the corn again being kept moist as
described above. The sprinkling is done to prevent the corn from drying
out and thus it is steamed and roasted at the same time. I have not as
yet had a word of complaint about corn prepared this way. But this is
not intended to be a "dissertation on roast corn." So let us move on to
our next fireplace.

RAISED FIREPLACE

The fireplace shown in Figure 77 is merely an adaptation of the surface fireplace just discussed. It has the advantage, however, of being elevated and thus makes stooping less of a problem. The bricks are laid flat. Any odd field stone or common brick can be used for the base. Loose brick laid in front of the fireplace will prevent embers from rolling out in front where the cook stands. The shelf is very handy for plates and utensils. All in all, this would constitute about as fine a fireplace as any. True, it is not quite as good as the pit type for a camp fire, but if fairly large, dry logs are placed in it in tepee fashion, you can get enough of a fire for all practical purposes.

As in previous chapters, I have given you what might be termed basic helps or suggestions. No doubt you have variations in mind that will prove very practical. For example, you might want more shelf area. Whatever the case may be, don't hesitate to launch right out with your ideas. A final suggestion might be made here. It might not be a bad idea to build your outdoor fireplace as soon as you have determined where the cabin is to stand. Thus you will get a great deal of use out of it when the cabin is being built.

HELP WANTED

Unless you are a superman and intend to do all the work on your log cabin by yourself, you will do well to consider the list of men whose assistance you would like to have. Perhaps friends will be willing to help you, or should I say, perhaps you are fortunate enough to know some good fellows who are willing to work. On the other hand, you may have to hire from one to three or four men if you are pressed for time. Whatever your employment situation proves to be, the following are the workers required to build a cabin.

ARCHITECT

If your cabin is going to be of a more pretentious type, you will very likely enlist the services of an architect. For the relatively simple dwelling that we have been discussing I hardly think that an architect will be required. From the instructions given herein you can plan almost any kind of small cabin by yourself. But you must use good common sense and know something about costs of and procuring material.

AX MEN

Here we do not have reference to loggers but rather to men who can handle a small hand ax. Most of the notching can be done with a hand ax. As a matter of fact there is very little chopping that requires a large ax unless the ends of the logs are to be chopped.

ADZ MEN

There is always a certain amount of adz work. Sometimes the smoothing out, or flattening, of logs for sills, rafters, and so on, can be done with an ax but a man who is handy with an adz can do the job a lot better and faster. A broad ax is sometimes used if the logs to be faced can be turned. An adz is also better than an ax for round notching, other things being equal.

SAWYERS

You probably think that anyone can saw a log in two. You are quite correct, but only one out of a dozen can make a straight cut. And remember, as we have pointed out previously, a straight cut is very essential at door and window openings.

CARPENTERS

Carpenters are very good to have around to make window and door frames, to square up sills and rafters, and to lay floors. And when it comes to making doors, a fellow with carpenter experience will prove a mighty valuable asset. He also has a lot of tricks up his sleeve for roof and porch construction.

DRAWKNIFER

This is another very important helper. The requirements of his job are long, powerful arms and ability to eye up a log and round it where necessary. Not everyone can handle a drawknife. When properly drawknifed, a log has the appearance of being freshly peeled. All peeled logs should be drawknifed if they are to be stained. Also, the inner side of old logs must be similarly shaved for staining. Log rafters can be leveled with a drawknife. Thus the drawknife proves to be a most essential tool and the drawknife man a most essential worker.

MASON AND CEMENT WORKERS

Don't ever get the idea that anyone can lay up a stone fireplace. Masonry is a trade and making a real fireplace is an art. Cement workers are not so essential except that they know what to do and how to do it in the shortest possible time—and time is a big item.

My father was a champion log sitter.

ELECTRICIAN

If electricity is available, you will undoubtedly make use of it. A good electrician will be very welcome, especially if the conduit or BX cable is to be laid in cement or plaster. Once laid, it is there to stay. Be sure to have him install a sufficient number of base plugs where you think they will be needed most.

PLUMBER

You probably have had little or no experience in installing plumbing so you had better get a plumber. If your cabin is to stand idle all winter, be sure that all water pipes can be drained properly.

LOG SITTER

Now we come to one of our most important helpers, the log sitter. Have you ever tried to saw a log without the help of someone to keep it from turning? Have you ever attempted to saw off the end of a log without someone to hold it to prevent splitting? Finally, have you ever tried to use an adz on a small log that was not steadied? If this has been your experience I am sure you will need no sales talk on the need for this valuable coworker. But the log sitter is more than his occupational classification implies for he is in fact a general handy man. He can do a hundred and one things around your cabin that others might consider unimportant. He is the fellow who will give you a lift when you need it. He is on hand to toss up that missing spike, to get that odd-size piece of lumber, and so on. Perhaps he can also cook up a good meal. So don't neglect him. He will be most useful from start to finish in all phases of construction.

This completes your staff. You probably won't need the help of all of these men at the same time. And then, too, it is very likely that some of them will qualify for more than one job.

Well worth the effort!

At this time I wish to thank the many friends who have helped me at this work and who have thus shared in a way in the production of this book. If I were to attempt to name them all there would be quite a list. They always were ready to lend a hand when the going was tough. Their ready wit, their willingness, their pride in doing everything right, their pleasantness made the job recreation rather than labor. Most of the fellows still drop in at the cabin to visit a moment or to spend an evening and I can't help thinking of the contribution each one made materially and socially. The old expression "a friend in need is a friend indeed" I suppose is a bit worn out at the cuffs but it certainly takes on fuller meaning after you have had the opportunity of working with a group of good fellows.

With wise planning, proper tools and materials, and pleasant, efficient help, building a log cabin can be a lot of fun. Moreover your efforts will be more than amply rewarded, for you will have something that will give unique enjoyment for many years to come.

RUSTIC
CONSTRUCTION

INTRODUCTION TO RUSTIC CONSTRUCTION

Practically everyone loves the appearance of things built up of rustic materials, in the rough-and-ready manner forced by necessity on our colonial forefathers. These hardy pioneers built their houses, barns, sheds, furniture, fences, gates, and bridges from materials which they found in, or wrested from, field and forest.

The things which they made in those early days can be made equally well today by any boy or man who loves to work with tools and wood. The gathering of the materials needed to make any type of rustic construction work will appeal specially to those who love the out of doors. Many of the things required may be found practically ready to hand in the fields, along the banks of rivers, on the shores of lakes, or in the woods and forests.

Modern machinery and hand tools will assist the craftsman of today to prepare articles of rustic construction with less effort than was required by the colonial pioneer doing the same type of work.

All of the various types of work described in this book have been actually made either by the author, or by craftsmen with whom he is acquainted. The designs shown cover a wide field of uses, and it will be found that they are not only pleasing to the eye, but that they also will withstand the ravages of the weather and the abuse of rough handling.

Photo by E. S. Shipp. Courtesy
U. S. Forest Service.

A slab about to be taken from a log in a
portable saw mill.

SLAB FURNITURE

MATERIALS

Slabs are the trimmings left after squaring up logs into lumber. See Figure 1. In rural districts, there are portable sawmills to be found, where farmers have their logs sawed. Around these mills one can usually find a pile of slab wood from which choice pieces for making slab furniture may be selected.

If one lives in the city, there are always fuel companies that handle cordwood and slab wood, even in this day of oil burners.

The kind of wood varies, of course, with the locality. In the South, one may find slabs of cedar and cypress; in the West, redwood and fir; in the northern states, oak, birch, pine, bass, and the like.

If the furniture to be made is to be left out of doors, oak, cypress, pine, and cedar are the best. If it is to be used in a log cabin or on the porch, any light wood will do. The lighter the wood for indoors, the better, because then the furniture may be made of thicker slabs and will look much sturdier than if made of a thinner hardwood slab. The city fuel dealers will usually allow one to go over the piles of slab wood and pick out suitable pieces. The slabs are cut 4 ft. long. In rural districts and at all sawmills, the length varies with the length of the logs brought in. However, 4 ft. is a good length for benches and tables.

Pick out slabs that run from 12 to 18 in. wide and from 3 to 6 in. in thickness at the thickest part. The bark, of course, is to be left on in order to add beauty to the finished piece. If benches with backs are to be made, pick out a few slabs about 6 in. wide and about 1½ in. thick.

Fig. 1. The rough slabs.

Fig. 2. Saplings.

Saplings (Fig. 2) for legs, arms, and stretchers, also are needed. Here again the different localities yield different kinds of wood. If the saplings must be cut by the person using them, a trip into the country where woods and roadside brush abound is in order. Permission should, of course, be obtained from the owner before felling the saplings, and then the limbs and tops should be placed in heaps and not scattered all over the woods. Where tamarack swamps abound, farmers often cut poles in winter and stack them up. These are sold for various purposes, such as fence posts, gateposts, hay poles, etc. In many such places, saplings may be purchased for a reasonable price.

If tamarack is obtainable, it will be found easy to work. Saplings should run from 1 to 3 in. in diameter, depending on where they are to be used. If no tamarack is obtainable, any solid saplings will do. Ironwood, elm, ash, or any wood of a tough character free from knots or at least straight, may be used. The branches and knots can be trimmed off if need be. The saplings may be peeled or left with the bark on. Since slab furniture is not made of measured lumber, the dimensions given in this book are only general.

If slabs are not readily obtainable, this type of furniture may be made of softwood planks from 2 to 3 in. in thickness and from 12 to 16 in. in width. These, of course, would be purchased at a lumberyard and should preferably be of pine, or other softwood. The legs for plank furniture may be made by slightly rounding off 2 by 2-in. pieces of the same wood. The method of constructing plank furniture is practically the same as that used for building furniture with slabs and saplings.

TOOLS

Most of these rustic pieces may be made with an ax and a bit and brace, but other tools, such as the hand crosscut saw or bucksaw, a sharp hand ax, a drawknife, spokeshave, expansive bit, jack plane, a few chisels, a hammer, and a mallet will make the work very much easier. If one is handy with or owns an adz, so much the better. Slabs finished with a sharp adz and sanded have a wonderful appearance.

PREPARATION OF THE MATERIAL

The preparation of slabs depends upon individual choice or ability. Some manufacturers of slab furniture run the cut side of the slab over a

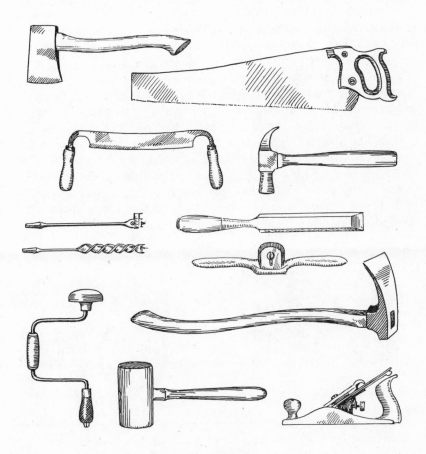

Fig. 3. A good selection of tools.

Fig. 4. The slab ready for use.

jointer and then sand it. That looks very commercial and is not consistent with the bark that is left on the other side. Others run them over a jointer to level them and then plane them by hand to give them the proper touch. Another way—and this is the one usually used by the writer—is to plane off only enough of the rough sawed surface to get it smooth, leaving a trace of the saw marks. The large-toothed saws, especially circular saws, used for sawing lumber leave a rough surface with millions of splinters. After planing off the rougher portion, it is usually necessary to sandpaper the surface to remove these splinters. The edges and ends should be cut as shown in Figure 4. Edges and corners are rounded with a drawknife or spokeshave.

When slabs with rough bark are used, it is advisable to trim down the rougher part of the bark with a drawknife. White pine, hemlock, and tamarack bark when shaved off produce a surface of rich reddish brown interlaced with purple. The bark of yellow birch should be left as it is. The different woods found in different localities will need different treatment. However, when the bark is to be shaved down, lay the slab face down on a bench of some sort and clamp one end down, or nail a stop at the end nearest the worker. Then, with a drawknife, take off just enough of the rougher bark to give it a nice appearance. See illustration.

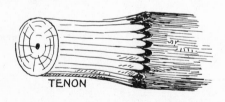

TENON

Fig. 5.

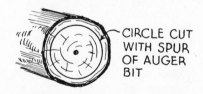

CIRCLE CUT
WITH SPUR
OF AUGER
BIT

Fig. 6.

Frequently, after slabs have been subjected to rain and snow, the bark loosens. This may be remedied by tacking the loose pieces down with shingle or lath nails after all work with the drawknife and bit is finished. Simply drive the nails wherever needed, then leave the slabs outdoors for a night or so, so that the nailheads will rust and in that way blend with the red or brown bark. If the bark is oiled before the nails are rusted, the heads will always appear unsightly.

CONSTRUCTION OF FURNITURE

The first thing to do in making the legs is to select one or more suitable saplings. Choose four pieces 17 in. long or longer and trim off all extending parts where limbs have been chopped off. This may be done with a knife or a spokeshave. Next, decide what size tenons are to be cut. As a rule, a little more than the bark of the piece having the smallest diameter is to be cut away. See Figure 5. Then set an expansive bit to bore a hole to fit this tenon. The other three legs are then marked with the bit as is shown in Figure 6. The holes in the slab must be bored with the same setting of the bit.

There are three ways in which legs or tenons may be fastened. Of course, if both the slab and the saplings used are well seasoned, one can simply put glue on the tenon and drive it home. But this is not the case in most instances. Therefore, it is well to use other means of fastening.

If a snug fit has been made, the leg may be driven home, and a large nail or spike driven in at an angle, as shown in Figure 7. This will do the trick, but there is no way of ever tightening such a leg should it loosen, except by driving another spike into it at another angle.

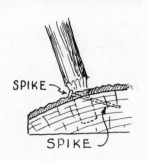

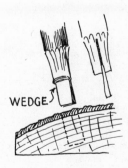

Fig. 7.　　　　　Fig. 8.

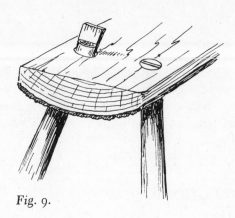

Fig. 9.

The blind-wedge method shown in Figure 8 is another way. The tenon should be fitted first; then a slot about 1½ in. deep is sawed at right angles to the grain of the wood, and a wedge of hardwood cut to fit. The wedge is then set into the slot and the leg driven in place. The wedge spreads the end of the tenon and holds it firmly. When green saplings are used, another method may be employed by boring the hole from the top of the slab all the way through, as is shown in Figure 9. If this method is used, the tenon is cut so that about ½ in. protrudes through the hole. Remove the leg and saw a slot down the center of the tenon and again drive it in place. Then drive a wedge in from the top and saw it off flush with the seat. Then when the wood dries and the legs loosen, the wedge may be driven in farther or a thicker wedge put in place of it. Where slabs are quite thick, holes may be bored and dowels driven in, as shown in Figure 10.

To fasten the rungs, use nails as was done for fastening the legs, or bore holes through them and tie them in place with rawhide thongs, as shown in Figure 11. The thongs should be cut ¼ or ⅜ in. wide and

Fig. 10.

Fig. 11.

soaked for about 12 hours before using. Pull them up as tightly as possible and conceal the ends. When the rawhide dries, it will shrink and hold for ages, provided no dampness reaches it. Varnishing it will help to keep dampness out. This method gives the furniture an added pioneer touch.

FINISHING SLAB FURNITURE

To finish furniture of this type, the first requirement is to bugproof the bark. A thorough brushing of 3 parts boiled linseed oil and 1 part turpentine will take care of this. If the furniture is to be left outdoors, do not use this oil on the worked surfaces of the slab, as it tends to turn dark in time. Outdoor furniture stands up better if the slab tops are given several coats of spar varnish. For indoor use a light coat of walnut stain, thinned down with turpentine and a coat or two of shellac or varnish will do very nicely on the raw wood. The bark on indoor furniture, too, should be given a good brushing of linseed oil and turpentine.

Sometimes the legs, rungs, and stretchers are made of peeled saplings. If the bark does not peel readily, it may be cut away with a drawknife. These peeled rounds should be finished the same as the slab tops.

MAKING A BENCH

Select the slab that is to be used for the seat. Since the legs of these benches are usually set at an angle, it is well to make a jig, such as is shown in Figure 12, to act as a guide in boring the holes. The distance

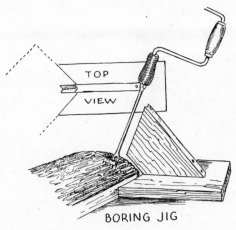

TOP VIEW

BORING JIG

Fig. 12.

that the leg is set in from the edge and end of the slab depends upon the conditions. With thin slabs, it is best to bore the holes farther from the edge than on thicker slabs. For the average slab, the center of the hole should be about 4½ in. from the end and from 2½ to 3 in. from the edge. The angle on the boring jig should be between 15 and 20 degrees.

Assemble the bench as has already been described. After the legs have all been fastened into the slab, the bench will require leveling. Set it on a level table or on the floor and level it up with small pieces of wood placed under the shorter legs as shown in Figure 13. Then use a piece of lumber of the right thickness as a saw guide (see Fig. 13). Saw half-way through each leg; then turn the bench on its side and finish sawing off each leg.

Fig. 13.

Fig. 14.

MARK ON
INSIDE OF
LEG TO
SHOW WHERE
TO BORE

MARKS TO SHOW
ANGLE AT WHICH
TO BORE

LENGTH
OF
RUNG

Fig. 15.

If rungs and stretchers are used, they should be thinner than the legs and the holes, and tenons should be 1 in. or even smaller if small saplings are used. When making a bench with rungs and stretchers, bore the holes, fit the legs and level off as before mentioned. Mark each leg as shown in Figure 14 with yellow crayon, so that it can be put back in the same position. Measure up 6 to 7 in. from the end of each leg and mark. Then place a rule as shown in Figure 15 and draw a line along it. This gives the proper angle for the boring. Then mark the place on the inner side of each leg to show where to bore. Lastly, measure how long the rung is to be, measuring from the center of each leg, as shown in Figure 15. When ready to assemble, fit the legs and rung together first. Then drive the legs into the seat or slab, and fasten everything. Rungs, as a rule, need no special fastening, but a ⅜-in. dowel or a nail will always help to keep them in place, especially when the bench is to be left outdoors.

If a stretcher is to be added (see Fig. 16), fit the legs and rungs on each end temporarily and then measure the length of the stretchers. As the rungs may be turned without changing anything, bore the holes for the stretcher ends in the center of each rung without any special marking.

Fasten two lengths with their rung in place at one end of the bench. Then assemble the other two legs with the rung and stretchers. Set them in place and drive everything together solidly. Dowels or nails may be used to fasten the ends of the stretchers.

Fig. 16. Slab bench with rungs and stretcher.

Fig. 17.   Slab bench with back.

Fig. 18.   Slab bench and chair.

BACKS

Figures 17 and 18 show a bench with back and armrests. The arm-rests may be left off, but they add considerable strength to the back. Figure 19 shows front and end views of such a bench. Note that the arms are set out farther to the edge of the seat, and should be set at a slight angle outward and forward. Smaller slabs are used for the back, and if one can be found with a curve to it, so much the better. The side view shows how the back is set into the upright.

The uprights are fastened into the slab just as is done with the legs. Then the back is simply set in and nailed on. Two narrow slabs may be used for the back instead of one wider one.

Figures 20 and 21 show another method of fastening back and armrests to the bench.

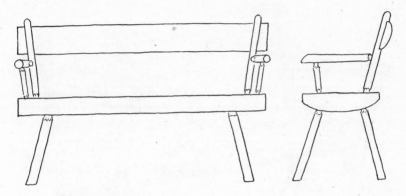

Fig. 19. Method of construction.

Fig. 20.

Figures 22 and 23 show examples of what might be called half-log benches. The logs for benches of this kind are usually obtained from trees that have been blown down, or that have died.

Fig. 21.

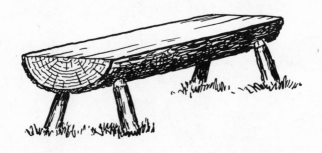

Fig. 22.

Fig. 23.

The good sections of such trees may be sawed out and the logs thus obtained sawed down the center, lengthwise. If there is no sawmill available, the log may be split by using wedges. The portion to be used as the seat of the bench must then be smoothed down with an adz.

The legs are put into these half-log benches as already described. Because of the weight of these benches, they are usually placed where they do not have to be moved very often.

Short logs or slabs may be utilized for making small benches or stools like the one shown in Figure 24.

Fig. 24.   Short bench or stool.

Fig. 25.

TABLES

Rustic tables are usually made for outdoor use and therefore should be made of wood that will withstand the weather. For indoor tables, use the lightest wood to be found such as bass, pine, or some other light local wood. Tables are usually 30 in. high, while top sizes depend upon what they are to be used for, and the material that is procurable or on hand.

Table tops should be planed down quite smooth. They are usually finished with two or more coats of spar varnish. Figure 25 shows a table made from a single wide slab. (In the author's locality, a wide slab is about 20 in. wide and about 5 in. in the thickest part.) The table is made as though it were a bench, 30 in. high. The legs for such a table should be about 3 in. in diameter at the thickest end.

Figure 26 shows another single-slab table. The advantage of the lower structure of this table is that the legs will not sink into soft ground. The uprights are mortised into the top and set into the lower crosspieces. The crosspieces are logs split or sawed in half. The braces shown in the illustration may be fastened with nails or spikes as shown.

When a wider table is wanted, use two or three slabs for the top. To make a table of the type shown in Figure 27, plane the slabs to a smooth surface, and cut the edges square and straight. A piece of 4-in.

sapling ripped down the middle will make satisfactory crosspieces. To fit the crosspieces, place the slabs, smooth side down, side by side, with the crosspieces in place. Mark the location of the crosspieces with yellow crayon. Saw along these marks to the depth shown in Figure 28; then cut out the dado with a wide chisel. Measure the remaining wood at each edge to make sure that the top pieces will be even. Before nailing the crosspiece in place, determine where the legs are to be placed and mark. Then proceed to nail, spike, or screw the crosspiece in place. If the top should not be even, a little planing will soon

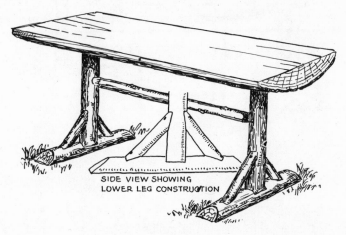

SIDE VIEW SHOWING
LOWER LEG CONSTRUCTION

Fig. 26.

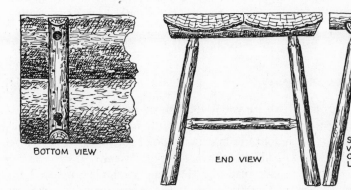

BOTTOM VIEW

END VIEW

SIDE
VIEW
OF
LEG.

Fig. 27.

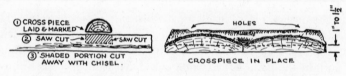

Fig. 28.

Fig. 29.

remedy the trouble. The table top is then ready to be placed on any sort of base. Figure 27 shows a simple method. The legs are made of 3-in. saplings.

For a table of the type shown in Figure 29, smaller saplings may be used for the legs. It will be found that 2 or 2½ in. will do nicely, with a 4-in. sapling for the lower crosspieces. Care should be taken in fitting this table together to get it an even height. A slight unevenness may be remedied by shaving off some of the bottom side of the crosspieces.

CHAIRS

Chairs require slabs that are wider than those used for benches. It is well, therefore, to save the wide slabs especially for the purpose of making them. Chairs for indoor use may be made of softwood. Those to be exposed to the weather had better be made of hardwood.

Figure 30 shows a chair made by the same methods employed for making benches, except that the grain in the seat is made to run from front to rear, and that the back is made higher than those put on benches. The depth of the seat should be from 14 to 16 in., and the angle between seat and back from 100 to 110 degrees.

Fig. 30.   Fig. 31.

Figure 31 shows another type of chair, the seat and back of which are both made from the same 4-ft. slab. Cut the slab in two as shown in Figure 32. Next, cut the tenon on the longer piece, which is to be used for the back. This tenon should be 3 in. longer than the thickness of the seat slab and 3 in. wide. Slabs wide enough for chair seats are usually 3 to 4 in. thick, hence the tenon will roughly be about 3 in. square. Cut the shoulder at an angle of 70 to 80 degrees, as shown in Figure 33.

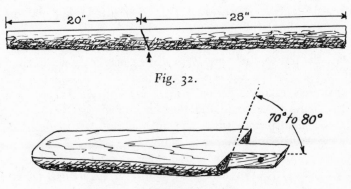

Fig. 32.

Fig. 33.

Fig. 34.

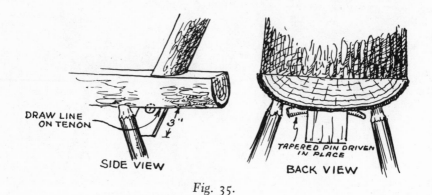

DRAW LINE
ON TENON

3"

SIDE VIEW

TAPERED PIN DRIVEN
IN PLACE

BACK VIEW

Fig. 35.

Measure back 14 in. from the front of the seat. See Figure 34, and cut a mortise to fit the tenon. Be careful to cut it at the same angle as that used for the back. Then assemble the back and seat, and draw a line on the tenon to denote the thickness of the seat. See Figure 35. Take the two pieces apart again and bore a 1-in. hole through the tenon, using the line just drawn as the center, as shown in Figure 35. Next make a hardwood draw pin about 5 in. long, tapering from 1 in. to 7/16 in.

The legs should be set in place before fastening the back to the seat, as it is easier to bore the holes if the latter can be laid flat on the floor. Figure 31 shows the position for the legs.

The back is then set in place and the draw pin driven through the hole. Start the pin carefully and drive it in place as shown in the back view of Figure 35. This draws the back down firmly, where it will be held indefinitely in this position. When leveling up the legs, set the chair at a comfortable angle and then mark and cut them. The seat should slope slightly from front to rear, and the back legs should be given slightly more slant than the front ones.

A simpler method of making a slab chair is to fasten the back down to the seat with ⅜-in. lag screws as shown in Figure 36. Determine where the back is to be placed on the seat and bore two ⅜-in. holes through the seat. Then with the back held in place, bore ¼-in. holes into it to act as lead holes for the screws. These should then be screwed up solidly with a wrench. A short piece of sapling may be set against the back as an added brace, as shown in Figure 36.

Chairs of this type may be made quite comfortable by shaping the seat and the back as shown in Figure 37. This requires extra work with an adz or chisels but it is well worth the effort. This shaping must, of course, be done before the final assembling.

Figure 38 shows a chair made of bent limbs. It is rather difficult to find these natural bent limbs unless one is fortunate enough to be on hand when a large oak tree is cut down. But if one has the time and the place to look for them, many interesting things can be made with

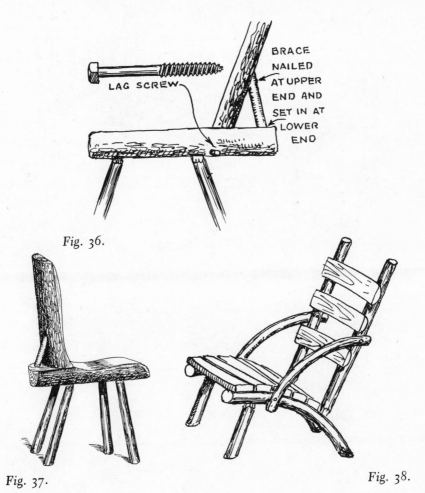

Fig. 36.

Fig. 37.

Fig. 38.

123

them. In the chair shown, there are two cross stretchers which are not seen after the seat is nailed on. One is placed between the two curved legs just forward of the front legs, and the other across beneath the last seat slab. These stretchers should be mortised.

BEDS AND COTS

Saplings may also be used for making beds and cots. Figures 39 and 40 show two types of so-called rope beds. This name has been given to these beds because rope is used in place of the bedsprings. If regular bedsprings are to be used in one of these rustic cots, it is best to buy the spring first, and then build the bed around it. Three-quarter and

Fig. 39.

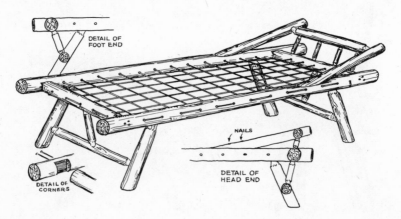

DETAIL OF
FOOT END

NAILS

DETAIL OF
CORNERS

DETAIL OF
HEAD END

Fig. 40.

double-size beds may be made in the same way as these single cots shown in Figures 39 and 40.

The saplings or poles used for these rustic cots should be from 3½ to 4 in. diameter. Tamarack poles, with their sturdy stiffness, are ideal for this purpose. Cedar and spruce also may be used. The poles should be peeled. The bark is most easily removed from saplings felled in spring. Those cut at other seasons usually require a drawknife for the peeling process.

A light coat of walnut stain thinned with turpentine will help to take the newness from the saplings used on these cots. A coat of flat varnish on top of the stain then finishes the job.

These cots may be made from 6½ to 7 ft. long, 2½ to 3 ft. wide, and they should be 15 to 16 in. high from the floor to the top of the side pieces. This height is desirable, because it makes the cot useful also for seating purposes.

New manila rope, ¼ or ⅜ in. in diameter, spaced 4 to 5 in. apart, may be woven back and forth as shown in Figures 39 and 40, to take the place of the modern bedspring. A piece of canvas may then be laid over the ropes, before placing the straw or cornhusk mattress upon them. If a regular mattress is used, the cot should be made so that the mattress will fit snugly between the side pieces. Some army or Indian blankets, sheets, and a pillow then complete these rustic beds.

The cot shown in Figure 39 may be used both for sleeping purposes and as a daytime lounging seat.

The cot shown in Figure 41 shows slightly different construction from that pictured in Figure 40.

Fig. 41.

125

16 INTERIOR FIXTURES AND EQUIPMENT

SHELVES

As has been stated before, slabs may be used in the same manner that one would use boards. They are, therefore, also useful for building shelves.

The simple shelves shown in Figures 42 and 43 are easily made and put up. The braces shown are of curved sections of branches. Straight pieces work equally well. For interior use, birch poles are very attractive. It should be remembered, however, that white birch poles are not

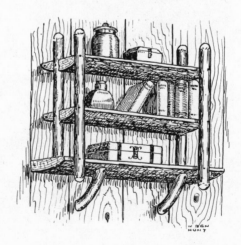

Fig. 42.

Fig. 43.   *Fig. 44.*

suitable for outdoor use and will not stand up well. Therefore, unless some tree or trees must be cut down to make room for something else, do not cut them for furniture in general. For ornamental things they will do very nicely, but a white birch certainly looks a lot better in the woods than anywhere else.

To put up a slab shelf, first fit the braces and brackets, secondly, nail them to the shelf or shelves, and then fasten the assembled pieces in place with nails through the ends of each shelf into the wall. Then drive one nail at the bottom of each bracket.

Figure 44 shows how fungi may be used for making a wall whatnot.

CANDLESTICKS

It was the author's good fortune to be present at a camp in northern Michigan when some white birch trees of about eight inches in diameter had to be cut down to make room for a roadway. As these logs were too beautiful to be used for firewood, something worthwhile had to be thought up. Some of the logs were carefully put in a dry place and one large log was peeled and the bark laid flat with some stones on the top to keep it from curling. The lamps and candlesticks shown and described here were then made.

Figure 45 shows a very simple and easily made candlestick. Of course, no definite dimensions need be adhered to in making these candlesticks. Some are tall, others short, some are off center at the base; every one is different.

It is easiest to make them of greenwood. The part marked *B* in

127

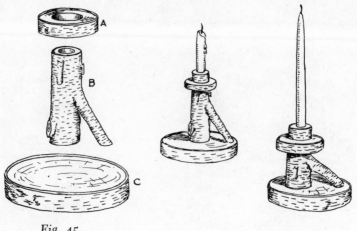

Fig. 45.

Figure 45 may be from 1¼ to 2 in. thick and the parts A and C in about the proportion shown. The base C is fastened to B with two or three finishing nails. The branch which forms the handle need not be fastened. The drip cup A, if fitted snugly, will hold without fastening, otherwise a few finishing nails will hold it in place securely. Figure 46 shows how a fungus growth may be turned into a good-looking sconce or candleholder. Since these fungus growths are quite inflammable, it is advisable to use sconces and candleholders made of them for decorative purposes only.

Fig. 46.

LAMPS

The birch lamp shown in Figure 47 is quite similar in construction to that used for the candlestick just described. This lamp is to be wired for electricity. Birchbark lamp shades may be made for kerosene or gasoline lamps also, but care should be taken not to have the birchbark too close to the chimney as it is resinous and very inflammable.

To make the lamp shown in Figure 47, cut the pieces as shown and bore ⅜-in. holes through the centers. Then cut the feet, which are 1-in. pieces cut at an angle. Glue the feet to the base and fasten with a couple of brads. The three pieces A, B, and C are then held together with a piece of ⅛-in. iron pipe, with the socket at the top and a nut at the bottom. Figure 48 shows the lamp completed.

Figure 49 shows a lamp in which the piece A, shown in Figure 47, was made larger. Small pieces of cherry twigs of ½-in. diameter were then used as shown. Cherry bark is similar to birch except that it is a shiny dark reddish brown. The contrast between it and the white birch makes it very attractive.

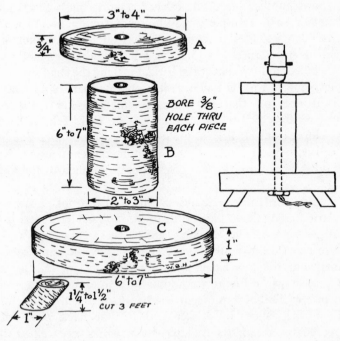

Fig. 47.

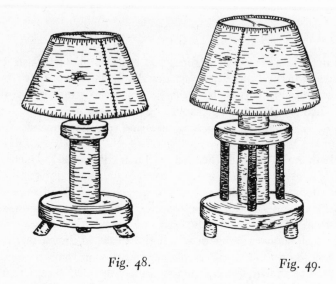

Fig. 48.   Fig. 49.

The cherry twigs are set in holes bored in A and C, Figure 47, and the whole lamp is assembled at one time. The lamp shown in Figure 49 also shows another piece set above A (shown in Fig. 47) of the same diameter as B. This piece may be made from 1 to 1½ in. high.

Birchbark lamp shades are somewhat difficult to make. Not only is the birchbark stubborn stuff to handle, but it is also frequently necessary to use two or more pieces of the bark in making the shade.

Freshly stripped bark is much easier to work than bark which has dried. As it is seldom that one makes a thing like this in the woods, keep the bark flat until ready to use and then soak it in water for a few days before using. If heat is applied evenly to the inner side of the bark it will flatten out nicely. Birchbark from cold climates has lichens growing on it. Leave this on as it gives a pleasing touch to the finished article.

The simplest way to make shades of this kind is to take apart an old paper or parchment shade measuring 10 in. in diameter at the bottom and 6 in. at the top. The two rings are to be carefully laid aside for they are to be used on the new shade. Then, using the paper as a template, mark out the two halves with a scratch awl or pencil on the birchbark, as shown in Figure 50. Add an inch to each half and cut out the two pieces. The next problem is what to sew with. The Indians sewed their birch canoes and baskets with fine tamarack roots, but this sewing material is not always available. Raffia works very well. It should be kept moist while sewing. Use an ordinary darning needle. The two halves are to be sewed together as shown in Figure 51, after which the bark should be bent so that the other two edges may be sewed together.

Then set the rings in place and sew them as shown in Figure 52 using one short and one long stitch. This prevents the bark from splitting so readily and tends to ornament the edges at the same time.

Birchbark shades may also be made for kerosene lamps, but a different arrangement must be used to hold the shade. Either three wire hooks are used, as shown in Figure 53, to fit over the upper edge of the lamp chimney or the arrangement shown in Figure 54 is used to support the shade.

Template laid on bark and marked, an inch being added to each half for overlaping.

Fig. 50.

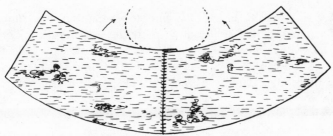

Fig. 51.

Fig. 52.

Fig. 53.

Fig. 54.

CANDELABRA

Figure 55 shows a very simple candelabrum which may be made of any straight poles. Wild cherry is a beautiful wood for this purpose. The standard should be about 5 ft. high, the arms about 14 in. long, and for the base a piece of slab wood 1 ft. square will prove satisfactory.

The cups and drip pans may be made of sections of larger pieces of wood, or common tin candlesticks may be fastened onto the arms with a couple of small brads.

The hanging fixture shown in Figure 56 is made of 3-in. tamarack. Cut the saplings in half, and join them at the center with a lap joint. As with the candelabrum shown in Figure 55, common tin candlesticks or heavier wood candlesticks may be used. The candlesticks should be made to hold large plumber's candles. The pendants are pine cones. Four 1-in. screw eyes are screwed into the tops. These must be opened just enough so as to admit the end links of the chain.

This fixture should be suspended from the ridge pole.

To electrify it, flat wire tape should be run along the upper flat surface, and the lead-in wires should be run through the links of the chains. A pull switch may be set into one of the arms, and a small pine cone may be used on the end of the pull chain or cord.

Figures 57 and 58 show how fungi may be used as electric-lighting fixtures. These fungus growths may often be found while walking through the woods. If handled right, many pretty and useful things can be made out of them for camp, cottage, or cabin. A fungus measuring from 10 to 12 in. in diameter will make a unique center-light fixture like the one shown in Figure 57. One or more electric-light sockets may be set into the bottom and the fixture can be fastened to the ceil-

Tin candlestick

Top view

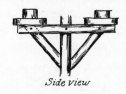

Side view

Fig. 55.

Fig. 56.

Fig. 57.

Fig. 58.

133

ing with three saplings or some odd-shaped branches, or it may be suspended by three pieces of old iron chain.

Other useful and ornamental things also can be made of these strange growths. Two fungi of somewhat the same shape and size, for instance, may be made into book ends by fastening them to pieces of old weathered boards, as shown in Figure 59. Fungus from hemlock logs and stumps is beautiful for this purpose as both the top and bottom surfaces are a beautiful glossy dark brown. The part that was attached to the log is simply trimmed off straight and fastened to the board with a few brads.

When handling fungi other than that from hemlock, care should be taken not to mar or scratch the bottom or light side as it quickly turns brown in those places. It is this peculiarity that makes them valuable as souvenirs of hunting, camping, and fishing trips, as one may use any sharp point to scratch names, dates, places, and the like on the white soft surface. These scratches will immediately turn brown and will keep indefinitely. Figure 60 shows such a piece of fungus decorated with a sketch of a camp. This memento of a fine vacation was made by the author many years ago, and it is still in very good condition.

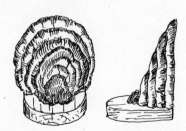

Fig. 59.

Fig. 60.

FENCES AND GATES

FENCES

Only general dimensions can be given for the guidance of those who want to build rustic fences. Fence posts are usually 6 ft. long. They are set 2 ft. into the ground, and are usually 4 to 6 in. at the butt end. The poles used for horizontal members should be from 2½ to 3 in. in diameter, and the crosspieces should be slightly smaller.

Fence posts will naturally rot and decay in time, but this may be prevented to a great extent by brushing creosote on that part of the post which is to go into the ground. A better way of preventing decay is to peel the bark off that part of the posts which is to go underground and then set the posts into a barrel containing just enough creosote to cover the portion of the post to be treated.

Another method that may be used for protecting the posts against decay is to char the part that is to go into the ground. To do this, build a good fire and lay several posts on it, turning them from time to time to get an even char.

Where a fence is built only for ornament and where the ground is not too hard or stony, fence posts may be pointed and driven into the ground with a beetle. Figure 61 shows how a beetle is made. The head of the beetle should be made of ironwood or some other hardwood that can stand severe punishment. The two iron bands should be shrunk on, preferably by a blacksmith. Do not use an iron sledge as it invariably spoils the top of the post.

Set the fence posts first. Then notch them, and fit and nail in the

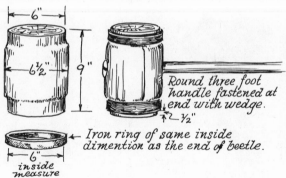

Round three foot handle fastened at end with wedge.

Iron ring of same inside dimention as the end of beetle.

inside measure

Fig. 61.

horizontal poles. After that, locate where the crosspieces are to come, cut the notches, and fasten the pieces in place with nails.

While a rustic fence may look more picturesque if the bark is left on the poles, nevertheless, this bark will soon begin to loosen and peel off. Then, too, there is the additional danger that insects may get under the bark. If tamarack poles are used, the loose bark should be scraped off, as shown in Figure 62. Then a mixture composed of 3 parts linseed oil and 1 part turpentine should be brushed over the poles to keep off the insects.

Fig. 62.

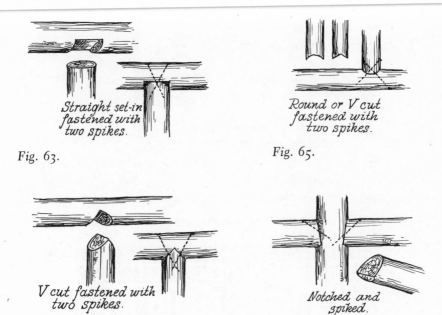

Straight set-in
fastened with
two spikes.

Fig. 63.

Round or V cut
fastened with
two spikes.

Fig. 65.

V cut fastened with
two spikes.

Fig. 64.

Notched and
spiked.

Fig. 66.

Those who like the appearance of peeled weathered poles will find that after a year or so the peeled poles take on a beautiful gray tone. By that time the danger of injury from insects is practically over.

When choosing poles and posts for fences, be careful to pick only those that show no indications of decay. All joints on vertical pieces should be made as shown in Figures 63 and 64, at the top, while those used for the lower ends are to be made as shown in Figure 65 in order to avoid pockets where decay may start.

Figures 66, 67, 68, and 69 show how horizontal members and braces are notched, fitted, and fastened into place.

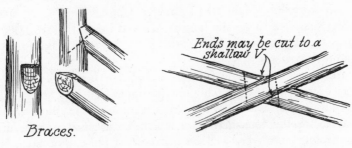

Braces.

Ends may be cut to a
shallow V

Fig. 67.

Fig. 68.

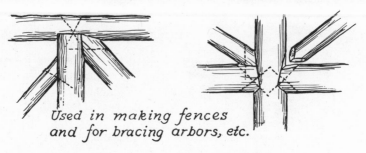

Used in making fences
and for bracing arbors, etc.

Fig. 69.

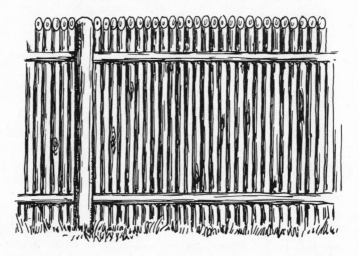

Fig. 70.

Figures 70 and 71 show how wattle fences are made. In some localities it is easier to obtain small straight saplings from 1 to 2 in. in
diameter than it is to get the heavier poles. If this is the case, the thing
to do is to make a wattle fence. Such a fence makes a beautiful back-
ground for a flower bed.

Wattle fences are made from 4 to 6 ft. in height. The poles are
either pointed or cut at a slant on the upper end, and straight across
at the lower end. They may be cut to a uniform height as shown in
Figure 70, or the tops may be left uneven as shown in Figure 71.
Cedar saplings serve very well for this type of fence. The poles should
be nailed to horizontal members consisting of two-by-fours or heavier

Fig. 71.

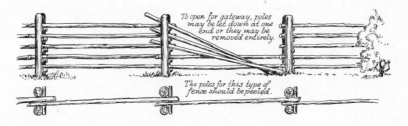

To open for gateway, poles may be let down at one end or they may be removed entirely.

The poles for this type of fence should be peeled.

Fig. 72.   Pole fence.

poles. One nail at the top and one at the bottom will be ample. Place every other sapling with the butt end up. This permits them to be spaced close together.

Figure 72 shows a simple pole fence. The crosspieces which are nailed to the uprights are made by splitting short lengths of pole. This type of fence may be opened at any point since the poles are not fastened at the ends.

The fence shown in Figure 73 is quite common in eastern Canada. It is picturesque, but takes time and energy to build. It has the advantage, however, that the uprights may be made in a shed or barn during the winter months, and the poles cut to the proper length. Then, when

139

Cut the openings large enough to hold the ends of two poles.

CANADIAN FENCE

Fig. 73.

spring comes, the uprights may be set the proper distance apart, the poles put in place and the fence is ready. The uprights for fences of this kind may be made of 2 by 6-in. yellow pine planks. The poles for fences of this kind should be peeled.

Making ornamental fences depends on several things; namely, the kind of poles obtainable, the purpose of the fence, its length, and the time one has to build it.

If the fence is to be both ornamental and useful, that is, if it is to keep out cattle, sheep, dogs, or chickens, then there are other things to be considered. The average 4-ft. fence will keep out cattle if built fairly strong, but for smaller animals the openings must be reduced. The pole fence and the Canadian fence may be made tight enough to keep out anything larger than a dog.

To keep out chickens one must fasten a wire netting along the inside and one or two strands of barb wire should be stretched along the tops of the fence posts to prevent cattle from reaching and people from climbing over. In fact, a fence is usually built to keep something out or keep it in, and must be built accordingly.

The fence shown in Figure 74 is a little harder to make than the straight rail type. Set the posts first and then the lower rail, which should be quite heavy. The two uprights marked A and B are then cut and fastened to the lower rail. A block of wood or the stone, shown in dotted lines, should then be placed. The top rail, which should be made of greenwood, is then laid across the tops of the uprights A and B and bent down. It takes two men to do this job. The notches having been cut in the posts, the ends are marked while bent, and then the pole is taken down and sawed off at the ends. Then it must be pulled

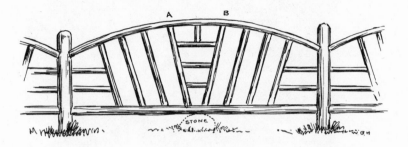

Fig. 74.

Fig. 75. Rustic fences.

Fig. 75. Rustic fences.

down and nailed down securely, after which the rest of the members are nailed in place.

The purpose of the stone under the center of the lower rail is to keep the lower rail from bending. These blocks or stones should be kept in place until the rails are thoroughly dry.

While a symmetrical fence may appeal to most people, there are fences that are not symmetrical and yet look very fine. Figure 75 shows examples of such fences. They may be built of more or less crooked limbs. Fences of this kind may be quite rough looking, but if the parts are consistently put together, the fence will be quite effective for keeping animals from breaking through.

Figures 76, 77, 78, and 79 show different designs that may be followed.

142

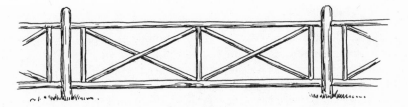

Fig. 76.

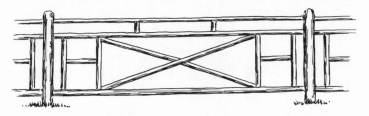

Fig. 77.

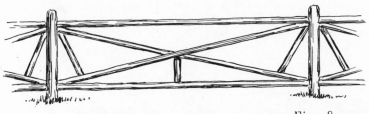

Fig. 78.

Fig. 79.

GATES

Gates usually get a lot of use. They should, therefore, be strongly made. The mortise-and-peg construction illustrated in Figure 80 should be used. Figures 81 and 82 show two different types of mortised gates.

Small gates, such as garden gates, should swing free; that is, the outer posts should not touch the ground. As these gates are subject to all kinds of weather changes, they naturally become loose in time and

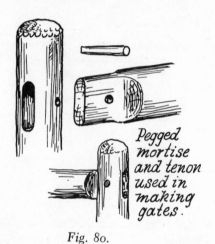

Pegged mortise and tenon used in making gates.

Fig. 80.

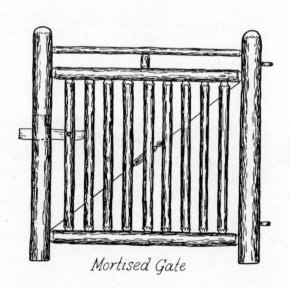

Mortised Gate

Fig. 81.

will have a tendency to sag. For this reason it is well to brace the gate or truss it. A wire with a turnbuckle will help matters if the wires are fastened at the upper hinge post and at the lower latch post, about where the crosspieces and the posts meet. See Figures 81 and 82.

The average garden gate should be about 4 ft. wide by 4 ft. high. Of course, if a gate is to permit a team of horses to go through, it must be wider, but a 4-ft. gate will permit passage of a good-sized wheelbarrow.

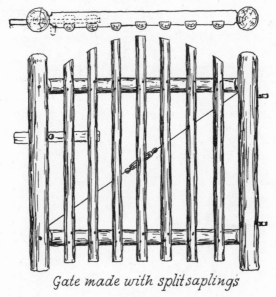

Gate made with split saplings

Fig. 82.

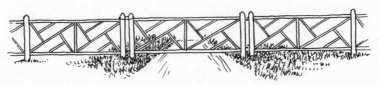

Fig. 83.

When a larger gate is used, it should be made like the rest of the fence as shown in Figure 83. Large gates may be made to swing free, but in that event, the gatepost into which the hinges are fastened must be heavier and set deeper into the ground. The hinges shown in Figure 84 are the easiest to fit, and they also permit the gate to be lifted off to be stored away. This sometimes is the easiest way of preventing temptation on Halloween night.

Where a gate is not opened often, it is easier to let the swinging end of the gate rest on the ground or rather on a flat stone when it is closed.

SCREW HINGES

Fig. 84.

Fig. 85.

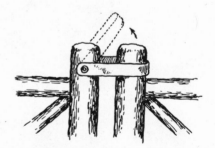

Fig. 86.

Figures 85 and 86 show two methods of fastening wide gates. The one illustrated in Figure 85 is a simple loop of iron which must be lifted off to open the gate. The one pictured in Figure 86 consists of a U-shaped iron band pivoted on the fence post so that it may be lifted and swung back to open the gate.

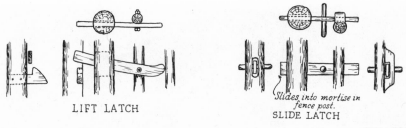

LIFT LATCH

Fig. 87.

SLIDE LATCH

Slides into mortise in fence post.

Fig. 88.

Figure 87 shows how to make a lift latch and Figure 88 pictures a slide latch, either of which may be made for use on the smaller gates.

Figures 89, 90, and 91 show other examples of how garden gates may be made.

Fig. 89.

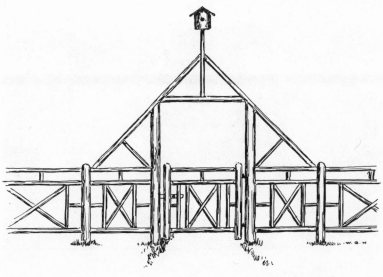

Fig. 90.

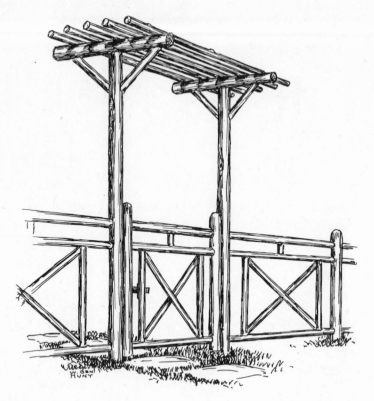

Fig. 91.

Smoothing the bark with a drawknife.

 **ARBORS**

Arbors may be made according to the directions laid down for fences and gates. While the rule to start out with thick poles and end up with smaller ones holds good for arbors too, a much more pleasing design will be obtained by using lighter poles as one goes up higher.

Fig. 92.

Fig. 93.

Figures 92, 93, and 94 show pleasing yet simple designs for three different kinds of arbors. Using these as samples, others may be designed. The arbors will naturally look as pictured when constructed. They will appear much more attractive, however, after the vines are grown over them.

The gateway shown in Figure 91 might also have been included in this section. While this gateway is not an arbor in the strict sense of the word, nevertheless, it takes the place of an arbor and it, too, will look very attractive after it is covered with a climbing vine, such as woodbine, wild grape, or bittersweet. The construction used in building arbors will, of course, be similar to that used in constructing fences and gates.

Fig. 94.

Fig. 95.

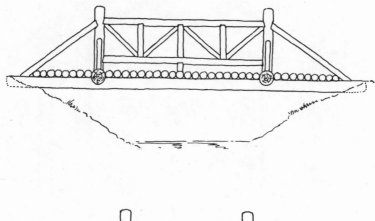

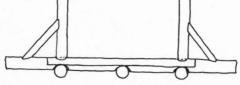

Fig. 96.
Top: Side view of bridge.
Bottom: End view of bridge.

BRIDGES

Figures 95 and 96 show the simplest kind of foot bridge, and illustrate the general construction. If the bridge is no wider than 3 ft., the center log may be omitted. If the bridge is to be less than 8 ft. long, 4- or 5-in. logs may be used for stringers. If the bridge is to be longer than 8 ft., heavier stringers must be used.

Fig. 97.

· Back of
Booth ·

Fig. 98.

20 WAYSIDE STANDS

Rustic wayside stands, if neatly built, always attract attention. The ones pictured in Figures 97 and 98 are of the simplest construction. They may be built entirely of poles, in which event tar paper is usually laid over the roof. The slabs are laid close together and show only from the inside and, of course, the ends of the poles should show also. The shelves used in these booths are made of planed or rough lumber. They should be set on an angle to show the produce better.

Figure 98 shows the interior arrangement of the stand. Flagstones laid in front as shown in Figure 97 not only improve the appearance, but also prevent the formation of a hollow which will catch and hold the rain, thus causing mud puddles where the customers are to stand.

The owner's sign painted on a slab may be fastened to the roof as shown, thus preserving the air of rusticity in every detail.

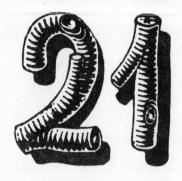

ROAD SIGNS

The road signs shown in Figures 99 and 100 are made of peeled poles or cedar posts, slabs being used for the roof. The sign itself is of dressed lumber and should be painted like any other sign. The poles are held together with lag screws. Two coats of spar varnish will give the signs a nice fresh appearance.

Fig. 99.

Fig. 100.

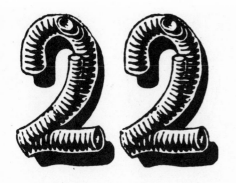

22 BIRD-HOUSES

When working with rustic material, a lot of odds and ends are usually left over. From this, very attractive birdhouses may be made. In walking through the woods, too, one occasionally finds hollow limbs or logs, which make fine birdhouses. Five slabs, culled from a pile of odds and ends, can easily be tacked together for a birdhouse resembling a hollow log. The required measurements for all ordinary birdhouses will be found at the end of this chapter. Cut four pieces of the slabs as long as the highest side of the house is to be, and nail them together about halfway up from the bottom in the manner shown in Figure 101. The pieces may also be nailed together as shown in Figure

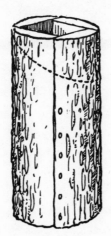

Fig. 101.

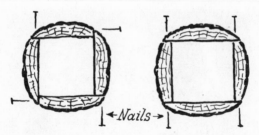

Fig. 102.

102. Bore the entrance hole according to the size shown in the chart, mark the slant of the roof, and saw off the surplus as shown in Figure 103. Then finish nailing up the sides. If some of the bark loosens, tack it down with lathing nails.

Next nail a piece of slab wood over the top for a roof, as shown in Figure 104. The roof may be left rough or it may be trimmed. A piece of board is next nailed to the bottom or fastened with four screws for easy cleaning. See Figure 105.

In making rustic birdhouses, do not be too fussy with fine trimmings. The houses should look as much like a hollow log as possible.

Do not place perches below the entrance holes as they are too much of a temptation for other birds to sit on while harassing the ones occupying the house. The type of house just described will do for wrens, bluebirds, and nuthatches, depending upon the size of hole and inside dimensions. For flicker and woodpeckers, the houses must be made longer, using the same construction.

Fig. 103.

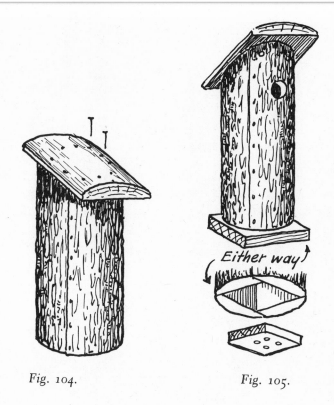

Fig. 104.   Fig. 105.

Holes should be bored around the upper ends of the sides and also through the bottom to allow for ventilation. One quarter to ⅜-in. holes will answer very nicely for this purpose.

A two-story wren house may be made by merely nailing a piece of board halfway up in a longer house as shown in Figure 106. This may be set in place before the fourth side is nailed on. Ventilating holes should be bored above and below this middle floor and also near the roof and through the bottom of the lower apartment.

A round, log-shaped house may be fastened to the top of a post with three pieces of 1-in. sapling, as shown in Figure 107, or it may be fastened to the trunk of a tree, with two pieces of sapling nailed to each side, and probably a small brace below. See Figure 108.

If the house is to be fastened against a building, the rear wall should be a piece of ⅞- or 1-in. board as shown in Figure 109. The roof should then be made to shed water to the sides. In other words, a gable roof should be placed on it. This is not as difficult as it looks. The four sides are nailed together as in the case of the first one described. See Figure 102. The house is then laid on the bench or "what have

159

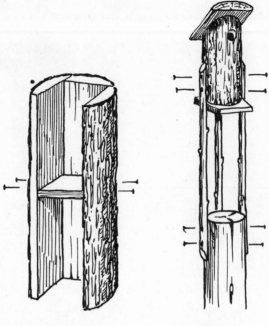

Fig. 106.   Fig. 107.

Fig. 108.   Fig. 109.

Fig. 110.

you," and the slant cuts are made as shown in Figure 110, cutting down to the backboard. The roof is then mitered as shown in Figure 109 and nailed on. If the miter doesn't fit as well as it should, whittle it flat at the ridge and nail a piece of sapling on for a ridge pole. See Figure 111. Don't forget ventilating holes.

Occasionally one finds a fine large piece of bark which is still solid enough for handling. A rough bird box can be nailed together and covered with this bark. Use nails that will not go through the box boards but they should be long enough to hold the bark.

Cedar bark makes a wonderful covering for birdhouses and at the same time furnishes a lot of nest material. Cedar bark can be obtained where cedar posts are peeled for fence or telephone poles. Old birch-bark is also a very good covering for birdhouses and will last for many years. Carpet tacks should be used for fastening on the birchbark, or small twigs may be nailed along the edges to hold it down. Figure 112 shows a birdhouse covered with birchbark.

Fig. 111.   *Fig. 112.*

Robin shelters also may be made of slab wood or saplings. Figures 113 and 114 show how this may be done. Robins will not nest in the ordinary type of birdhouse. For construction dimensions for shelters such as are shown in Figures 113 and 114, see the chart at the end of this section. Other types of birdhouses that are easy to make, and which birds like very much, are those made of hollow logs. Hollow logs and limbs may be found in almost every woods and frequently in stacks of firewood piled up in woods and pastures. This wood naturally belongs to some farmer, and when a hollow log is found in such a pile be honest enough to ask the owner if you may have it. As a rule these logs are not accepted as prime firewood and one may often have them for the asking. But don't forget to ask.

Fig. 113.

SIDE VIEW

Fig. 114.

Fig. 115.

These logs, measuring from 6 to 10 in. in diameter with their rotted-away insides naturally require some additional work. Cut sections 8 in. long for wrens and 10 in. long for bluebirds. Sometimes one slant cut will take care of two houses as shown in Figure 115. The rotted inner walls must be cut away with a chisel, leaving about 1 in. or so of solid wall. The entrance hole must then be bored, a top and bottom added, and presto, another wren or bluebird house is ready. Sometimes knot-holes make natural openings. Do not attempt to make a *beautiful* house, but rather a rough one that will attract birds.

Much could be written about rustic birdhouses and after reading it, and looking for hollow logs, probably the first one found would not fit any of the ones described in this book. The thing to do is to get the log, find out from the birdhouse dimension chart how large a house it will make, and for which birds it is best fitted, and then see what kind of house you can make of it. The writer once found half of a log measuring about 30 in. long and about 10 in. in diameter. The bark was off and the log was much weathered. It looked something like the one shown in Figure 116. After smoothing up the two side edges, it was cut into two pieces as shown in Figure 117. A board was then nailed over the back of the piece shown in Figure 118, and a piece of wood fitted and nailed into the lower end. Then a 10-in. square board was

Fig. 116.

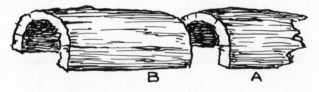

B A

Fig. 117.

Birds	Floor Space	Depth of Interior	Size of Opening	Height of Entrance from Floor	Height of House from Ground
Wren	4 in. square or 5 in. diameter	6 to 8 in.	7/8 in. diameter	About 5 in.	6 to 8 ft.
Bluebird	5 in. square or 7 in. diameter	8 to 10 in.	1½ in. diameter	About 6 in.	5 to 10 ft.
Robin	8 by 10 in.	8 to 10 in.	2 sides open		6 to 20 ft.
Tufted Titmouse	4 in. square or 5 in. diameter	8 to 10 in.	1¼ in. diameter	About 8 in.	6 to 12 ft.
White-breasted nuthatch	4 in. square or 5 in. diameter	8 to 10 in.	1¼ in. diameter	About 8 in.	10 to 20 ft.
Flicker	6 in. square or 9 to 10 in. diameter	12 to 15 in.	3 in. diameter	9 to 12 in.	10 to 25 ft.
Wood-pecker	6 in. square or 9 to 10 in. diameter	12 to 15 in.	1½ in. diameter	9 to 12 in.	10 to 25 ft.

nailed over the top, and a 1½-in. hole bored for the entrance. The remaining section was then nailed over the top and to the backboard as shown in Figure 119. This house has taken care of a bluebird family in the house proper, while a family of robins occupied the upper part for seven or eight years. The rough end was left just as it was on the log when found. This added to the natural look that birds like so well.

So far as known, no bird has ever measured up its prospective home with a rule or a tapeline. Nevertheless they are often very particular about entrance openings and the amount of room allowed them. It will be well, therefore, to follow the chart of birdhouse dimensions as closely as possible.

Fig. 118.   *Fig. 119.*

INDEX